27.95

Treating Lesbians
and
Bisexual Women

D1445716

Treating Lesbians and Bisexual Women

Challenges

and Strategies

for Health

Professionals

Elisabeth Paige Gruskin

SAGE Publications
International Educational and Professional Publisher
Thousand Oaks   London   New Delhi

For information:

SAGE Publications, Inc.
2455 Teller Road
Thousand Oaks, California 91320
E-mail: order@sagepub.com

SAGE Publications Ltd.
6 Bonhill Street
London EC2A 4PU
United Kingdom

SAGE Publications India Pvt. Ltd.
M-32 Market
Greater Kailash I
New Delhi 110 048 India

Printed in the United States of America

Library of Congress Cataloging-in-Publication Data

Gruskin, Elisabeth Paige.
    Treating lesbians and bisexual women: Challenges and
strategies for health professionals/by Elisabeth Paige Gruskin.
        p. cm.
    Includes bibliographical references and index.
    ISBN 0-7619-0044-6 (cloth: acid-free paper)
    ISBN 0-7619-0045-4 (pbk.: acid-free paper)
    1. Lesbians—Health and hygiene. 2. Lesbians—Medical care.
3. Bisexual women—Health and hygiene. 4. Bisexual women—Medical
care. 5. Medical personnel. I. Title.
RA564.87 .G78 1998
362.1'086'643—ddc21   98-25343

This book is printed on acid-free paper.

99 00 01 02 03 10 9 8 7 6 5 4 3 2 1

Acquiring Editor:	C. Terry Hendrix
Production Editor:	Wendy Westgate
Production Assistant:	Denise Santoyo
Typesetter/Designer:	Lynn Miyata
Cover Designer:	Candice Harman
Indexer:	Jean Casalegno

Contents

⤳ Preface

his book was conceived in the office of Bill Vega, my graduate school advisor. We were discussing the need for a reference to supplement the course on lesbian, gay, bisexual, and transgender health and culture that I developed and teach at the University of California at Berkeley. In his typically proactive fashion, my advisor suggested I put together a proposal, find a publisher, and write a book. Three years later, with the help of countless people, here it is.

This book is an integrated analysis of lesbian and bisexual women's health written for health professionals, including, but not limited to, physicians, nurses, therapists, counselors, and educators. The focus of the book is women who identify as lesbian or bisexual or women who are in sexual and intimate relationships with women. You will find, however, that much of the information is applicable to gay and bisexual men as well. For the most part, the concerns of bisexual women in relationships exclusively with men, although important, are beyond the scope of this book.

This book is based on experiences of both patients and health professionals directly communicated to me by my students, the speakers in my class, colleagues, friends, Internet acquaintances, and research subjects, as well as indirectly communicated through biographies, scientific articles, poems, anecdotes, documentaries, visual art, and presentations at conferences. Represented are a wide variety of people—from transsexual and young women who have spent portions of their lives living on the streets to the most financially secure elderly couples, most of their relationships having been secreted.

After you have read the book, you will, at the minimum, better understand how the lesbian and bisexual woman lives her life as it relates to her health and her health care. I sincerely hope you then will be able to contribute to the improvement of the health care system.

Acknowledgments

First and foremost, I would like to thank the many women whose experiences this book is based on; the students and speakers in my class, the women who I interviewed, and the many women who shared their experiences through literature, art, and film.

To the people who spent countless hours developing, reading, and rereading my work, the book would not be the same without you: Sheryl Fullerton, Sharon Ponder, and Carol Somkin.

Special thanks to my mother, who with every revision not only improved the book, but became more sensitive to and supportive of lesbians and bisexual women.

Bill Vega, your belief in me pushed my bounds beyond what I thought possible.

Carol Somkin, everyone should have someone like you in their life.

Carol Cohen, Margaret Schadler, and Magdelena, you helped keep me sane.

To my friends and colleagues at Kaiser Permanente for listening to me as I rambled on about the book and for supporting me in my quest to learn more about the health of lesbians and bisexual women.

Lynn Winters, Terry Taylor, Margaret Rosario, and Joyce Hunter for accepting me into their community.

C. Terry Hendrix and Dale Grenfell for giving me this chance to express my ideas and for facilitating the editing and peer review of the manuscript.

Thank you for the time and energy of those who peer reviewed the manuscript.

My family—
everyone should be so lucky. . .

◁ Introduction:
A Special Population With Special Needs

*W*hat is lesbian and bisexual women's health? Are not the health concerns of lesbians the same as those of all women? Bodies are bodies—why do lesbians and bisexual women need special consideration? I have heard health professionals and even lesbians ask these questions over and over. There are no easy answers because they involve more than just physiology, symptoms, and medical procedures. For health professionals to work with lesbian and bisexual women, they must understand the general hostility this population encounters in the general public and the medical establishment. They must appreciate the variety of life experiences of each individual woman and how they relate to their health and health care.

————— ℮ —————

Althea and Nancy

When Althea and Nancy met at a teacher's conference, both had had relationships with women, but Althea had not lived as a lesbian until she became involved with Nancy. Not only was she reluctant to tell her family about her relationships with women, but she also worried about the parents of the children she taught. They were uncomfortable enough with her being African American; if they found out about her relationships with women, she feared she would be forced to resign.

As their relationship progressed, Nancy became frustrated with what she felt was Althea's duplicity in her lifestyle and pressured Althea to tell her family about their relationship and to attend with her events in the lesbian and bisexual women's community. As tensions mounted over their differences, Nancy suggested they try couple's counseling.

Their first therapist, an "out" lesbian, in Althea's view, did not understand that her fear of coming out stemmed, in part, from the prejudice and racial discrimination she had experienced throughout her life. She felt much more comfortable, however, with their second therapist, an African American woman who helped both Nancy and Althea understand the complexity of coping simultaneously with racism and with the pervasive prejudices of a heterosexual world. As Althea became more secure in her relationship with Nancy, she came out to one of her sisters, and agreed to attend events in the lesbian community. Even so, it was still difficult for Althea, as she was one of the few women of color at most the events she attended.

Eventually, their therapist suggested they attend a conference for lesbian and bisexual women of color and read writings on the subject. At the conference, Althea had her first opportunity to talk with women she felt really understood her. Nancy, one of the few white women at the conference, began to understand how difficult it was to be in the minority. After she had listened to the presentations at the conference and read about the experiences of lesbians and bisexual women of color, she better understood the complexities of living with multiple identities. As Nancy became more supportive of Althea, Althea was able to acknowledge her fears and understand Nancy's frustrations.

Morgan

When Morgan had her first relationship with a woman in 1968 at the age of 22, she knew nothing about lesbianism, except that having sexual feelings for women was a sin and that she must not tell anyone. Coming out to her family a few years later supported her original fears. When she told them that she was a lesbian, they pleaded with her to pray for redemption and look to the church to help her stop her "sinful" behavior. When she refused and would not check herself into a psychiatric hospital to be "cured," they willed her out of their lives and insisted that her brothers and sisters sever their ties to her. She felt so guilty and isolated that she considered ending her life.

Eventually, Morgan found a supportive group of friends who socialized at the local lesbian bar, one of the only places where they felt comfortable being themselves. Morgan became a bartender. Her life at the bar revolved around drinking and socializing. She, like most of her friends, smoked heavily.

When the bar eventually closed, Morgan, then in her late 30s, went on unemployment and began looking for a new job. Assuming she was a lesbian, potential employers seemed uncomfortable with her "butch" demeanor. Behavior that had served her well in her former world somehow seemed wrong as she searched for new work. Although she did find another job within a few months, Morgan had lost her old sense of security. She became depressed and tried to cope; her drinking increased.

Not long after she found her new job, Morgan was attacked and beaten by a group of teenagers because they thought she was a "bull-dyke." While the police and medical personnel in the hospital emergency room responded indifferently to this hate crime, she turned for support to her lesbian and bisexual friends and to counseling at a gay and lesbian community agency. Not only did Morgan feel more vulnerable after the beating, but it left her with chronic back pain that she sought to self-medicate with even more drinking.

When she finally realized she had "hit bottom," Morgan checked herself into an alcohol treatment center. However, as the only lesbian, she felt uncomfortable when talking about her female partners and stigmatized by the other clients and staff.

As she was ready to leave the treatment center in despair, one of the nurses suggested that she attend a gay and lesbian Alcoholics Anonymous group. Her participation in the gay and lesbian program not only helped her stop drinking and change her life, but also enabled her to find a new network of "clean and sober" friends who understood and accepted her relationships with women. With this support system, she maintained her sobriety and found new balance in her life.

Janis and Marybeth

Janis, mother of 7-year-old Benjamin from her heterosexual marriage, and Marybeth, her partner of 4 years, decided they wanted to have a baby together and that Marybeth would give birth. Marybeth's health care plan covered artificial insemination only for women who were married to men. They saved enough money to go ahead with the process only to find that the sperm donor clinic in their town would not provide sperm to female couples or single women. Aware of the lack of legal protection for the nonbirth mother, especially when the father is known, they looked for and discovered a sperm bank in another nearby town that would provide sperm from an anonymous donor.

Although Marybeth's first Ob-Gyn provider said that she accepted lesbian relationships, her actions told another story. She never directly answered any of Janis's questions and she maintained eye contact only with Marybeth. They switched doctors three times before they found a doctor with whom they felt comfortable and who would treat them as coparents of their unborn child.

The couple had already looked into second-parent adoptions so that Marybeth could adopt Benjamin, but found that it was not legal in their state. They worked with a lawyer to protect their relationship with both of their children by legally changing all their last names to the same name, signing contracts that demonstrated Janis's commitment to raising the new baby and Marybeth's commitment to Benjamin, and signing agreements of joint custody in the case of a breakup. Both women granted each other durable powers of attorney for both health care and finances and they wrote new wills. They also had the members of their biological families sign an agreement prohibiting them from trying to gain custody of the children, if anything were to happen to either Marybeth or Janis. All of this legal maneuvering not only led to substantial attorney's fees but was stressful and difficult for them as a family.

Marybeth and Janis explained their situation and presented all their documents to each of their health care providers so that they would understand what to do in the case of an emergency. Even with these precautions, however, both Marybeth and Janis knew that there was a chance that either of them could lose custody of the children in the case of a breakup, or if the birth mother became incapacitated.

Laura

Laura, a transsexual lesbian, arrived at a shelter for battered women after surviving a particularly violent episode with her physically and emotionally abusive female partner. Two days after arriving at the shelter, a staff member, in a private counseling session, learned that Laura had not yet undergone genital surgery; she still had a penis. The staff decided that she posed a risk to other clients, even though there had not been any complaints, and forced her to leave. Laura's decision to make the transition to being a woman had already cost her all family support and was making it difficult for her to find a job and support herself. With nowhere else to go, she returned to her abusive partner.

The health concerns of the women you just met can only be understood by first considering the negative attitudes that lesbians and bisexual women confront at all levels: societal, institutional, and individual. Althea's relationship with Nancy was complicated by their differing perceptions of the risks of discrimination they faced as a result of disclosing their sexual orientation. The success of their therapy was dependent upon a therapist helping them work together to understand these differences. Morgan, from the beginning of her relationships with women, internalized society's negative attitudes to such an extent that she considered suicide and struggled with a lifelong drinking problem. The most direct manifestation of these negative attitudes, a hate crime, resulted in emotional trauma and physical injury. She also had difficulty finding employment and appropriate substance abuse treatment because of the way others perceived her gender and her sexual orientation. To treat her effectively, Morgan's health care providers had to understand the role that her own and her family's negative feelings about homosexuality played in increasing her health risks.

Janis and Marybeth had to overcome tremendous obstacles to conceive a baby and to protect their relationships with their children. Their health care providers needed to understand the legal and emotional ramifications of the process they were undergoing, as well as general discrimination against alternative family structures.

The decision not to allow Laura, the battered transsexual woman, to remain in a shelter stemmed from society's biases about the requirements for being a "real woman" or a "real man." Laura's injuries were much deeper than the physical symptoms of the battering she had received.

The health effects of these negative social and cultural attitudes were in turn influenced by who they were as people—including the identities they had constructed for themselves, the cultural norms of their social networks, their relationships with their biological families, their age, and their financial resources. As their life situations changed, so did the effects of discrimination on their health care and health. Similarly, each woman's financial security and family support contributed to the effect that discrimination had on them. Janis and Marybeth were fortunate to have the financial resources and family support that made it possible for them to minimize the effects of negative societal attitudes. On the other hand, because Morgan had little financial stability and no family support, she had difficulty coping with the discrimination she faced. Laura, who had been alienated from her birth family and had no financial resources, felt compelled to return to an abusive relationship. As with all patients, health care providers' understanding of their lesbian and bisexual patients' social support enhances their ability to assess their patients' risks, devise appropriate treatments, encourage clear and honest communication, and incorporate appropriate nonmedical supports in treatment plans.

In the pages that follow, you will meet women whose experiences will help you appreciate the complexity of lesbian and bisexual women's health. Their health can only be understood in the context of their lives, their experiences framed by the discrimination and bias they face, and the decisions they make based on all the other personal and societal factors. It is my hope that this book will help you better to understand your lesbian and bisexual patients and enhance your ability to provide them with the best care possible.

1

A Population at Risk

*T*he following are some of the health risks that lesbian and bisexual women face. The statistics are drawn from national and local studies. However, there are methodological considerations, including the problems of sampling, the relevance of older studies to a changing community, and the lack of universal categories and definitions. (See Appendix D for more information about lesbian and bisexual women's health research.) The implications of these statistics will be explored in more detail in subsequent chapters.

⤜ HEALTH RISKS

Hate Violence

During their lives, most lesbians and bisexual women experience hate violence such as verbal harassment, threats, vandalism, physical assault with or without weapons, and sometimes even murder. This puts them at risk for physical injury, symptoms of post-traumatic stress syndrome, and death. The stress from hate violence can also contribute to substance abuses or psychiatric symptoms (Herek & Berrill, 1992).

At least 2,212 people were victims of homophobic hate violence in 1994 in the 11 states which track these offenses (National Coalition of Anti-Violence Programs, 1996). In a study of lesbians and bisexual women in San Francisco, 84% were verbally harassed, 40% were threatened with physical violence, and 27% had objects thrown at them (Von Schulthess, 1992). In a review of 24 surveys of homosexual youth ages 15 to 24, 17% were physically assaulted, 44% were threatened with violence, 80% were verbally assaulted, 33% had objects thrown at them, and 31% were chased (data compiled by O'Hanlan, 1995).

Suicide

It appears that a disproportionate percentage of lesbians and bisexual women have attempted to end their lives as compared to heterosexual women. We do not know how many more have succeeded.

Paul Gibson (1989), in a report for the Secretary's Task Force on Suicide based on studies of gay and lesbian youth, speculated that gay and lesbian youth are two to three times more likely to commit suicide than youth who do not identify as gay or lesbian, and that gay and lesbian youth constitute up to 30% of all suicides. In 14 metropolitan areas 42% of gay youth attempted suicide (D'Augelli & Hershberger, 1993). In Chicago, 53% of lesbians at a gay, lesbian, and bisexual youth organization reported suicide attempts (Herdt & Boxer, 1993). In the first large-scale lesbian health study, 18% of the participants reported suicide attempts (Bradford & Ryan, 1988).

Stress

Lesbians and bisexual women experience unique stresses, in addition to the stresses all women experience (O'Hanlan, 1996). Stress is a health risk increasing the chance of myocardial infarction, asthma, diabetes, gastrointestinal diseases, and perhaps cancer, viral infections, and autoimmune system deficiencies. It may be a factor in substance abuse, unhealthy eating habits, and sleeping problems.

The stresses of lesbian and bisexual women include decisions about when to disclose their sexual orientation, hiding their sexual orientation, lack of support for their sexual orientation and relationships, absence of role models, identity development, and homophobia and heterosexism (Falco, 1996).

Mental Health

Lesbianism or bisexuality, in itself, does not result in psychological or personality problems. However, the little research that does exist indicates that the stress that lesbians and bisexual women face may lead to mental health symptoms such as depression, anxiety, or various forms of acting out, especially during the beginning stages of identity development (Ross, Paulsen, & Stalstrom, 1988).

Studies show that between 74% and 78% of lesbians and bisexual women use mental health services (Bradford, Ryan, & Rothblum, 1994). Commonly stated problems include depression, anxiety, loneliness, relationship problems centered around coming out issues, suicidality, and substance abuse.

Tobacco, Alcohol, and Food

The preponderance of research on lesbians and bisexual women indicates that they have a tendency to overuse alcohol, tobacco, illegal drugs, and have high levels of body fat. Hypotheses for these problems include the importance of lesbian bars for a social life, the use of substances to cope with stress, the social norms of the community, and the lack of culturally appropriate treatment centers for this population (EMT Associates, 1991).

In a study of adolescent lesbians and gay men, 33% reported excessive alcohol use and 23% reported illegal drug use (D'Augelli & Hershberger, 1993).

In a study comparing lesbians and bisexual women to heterosexual women, more lesbians and bisexual women used recreational drugs than did heterosexual women (Buenting, 1992). Among young lesbians and bisexual women from 14 metropolitan areas, 22% were concerned about excessive drug use and 26% were concerned about excessive alcohol use (D'Augelli & Hershberger, 1993).

In a study of lesbians and bisexual women in Northern California, only 35% were satisfied with their current weight and 15% reported a current eating disorder; 65% overeating, 16% bulimia, 10% anorexia, and 8% included both anorexia and bulimia (Gruskin, 1995). In another study of 203 lesbians, the rate of bulimia nervosa and attitudes concerning weight, appearance, and dieting was similar to that of heterosexuals.

However, the rate of binge eating disorder was more frequent than that
of heterosexuals.

Domestic Violence

Although there has been little research to date investigating same-
sex domestic violence, anecdotal and clinical experiences and the research that has been conducted indicate that female couples participate
in violent relationships at approximately the same rates as do heterosexual women (Elliot, 1996). Elliot (1996) reported the following in her
review of the literature:

1. In a study of 90 lesbians for Coleman's (1991) doctoral thesis,
   46% experienced repeated violence.

2. Physical aggression for conflict resolution was used by 46% of
   lesbians and gay men in the Kelly and Warshafsky study.

3. Of the 900 lesbians surveyed in the Twin Cities area of Minnesota,
   22% had been in a physically violent relationship.

4. In the Lesbian Battering Intervention Project Survey in Minnesota
   76% of the lesbian respondents had experienced some indirect
   threat of violence from a lesbian partner.

Cancer

Although there have not been any formal studies focusing on the
prevalence of cancer among lesbians and bisexual women, research
does show that lesbians and bisexual women may be at higher risk for
breast cancer, ovarian cancer, and colon cancer because they may have
more of the risk factors associated with these cancers. One risk factor
may be that lesbians tend to have fewer children than heterosexuals; two large studies showed that 74% to 85% had not had children
(O'Hanlan, 1996). Additional risk factors include higher body fat, several studies showed between 25% and 43% obesity (O'Hanlan, 1995);
high levels of substance abuse and smoking as previously discussed in
this chapter; and low rates of preventive care and screening.

◆ HEALTH CARE

Health Care Use

It appears that lesbians and bisexual women tend to use traditional health care less frequently than recommended. Many women access comprehensive preventive health care through family or contraceptive planning services. Lesbians and bisexual women are less likely to need reproductive services and often feel unwelcome at clinics providing reproductive health services (Banks & Gartrell, 1996).[1]

Studies show that the intervals between Pap smears are nearly three times longer for lesbians than for heterosexual women. A range of 5% to 10% have not had a Pap smear in the past 10 years (O'Hanlan, 1995). In a study of lesbians and bisexual women in Northern California, 50% did not have yearly Pap smears, fewer than one third had regular physicals, and 35% thought they should receive more care (Gruskin, 1995).

Barriers to Health Care

One of the barriers to health care for lesbians and bisexual women is finances. Studies indicate that they have lower income levels than would be expected based on their education level (Stevens, 1992). Lack of health care insurance is a particular problem because most lesbians and bisexual women cannot be covered on their female partner's health care insurance (Stevens & Hall, 1990). Barriers also include negative health care experiences and beliefs. Lesbians and bisexual women and many of their health care providers have the erroneous belief that they do not require gynecological screening (Peterson, 1996).

Health Care Experiences

Many lesbians and bisexual women report negative experiences with their health care providers after disclosure of their sexual orientation. In a study in Northern California, women whose providers knew their sexual orientation were more likely to be satisfied with their care and more likely to receive regular preventive care (Gruskin, 1995). In a study conducted in the Midwest, 72% of lesbians and bisexual women reported negative reactions to disclosure of their sexual orientation including; ostracism, shock, pity, invasive questioning, fear, embarrassment, mistreatment of partners and friends, breached confidence, rough physical handling, derogatory comments, and pathological assumptions (Stevens & Hall, 1990). In another study, 80% of elderly lesbians reported that they mistrusted health care providers (Deevey, 1990). In a study of lesbian and bisexual women, 50% delayed health care because of fears of mistreatment by health care providers (Zeidenstein, 1990). Stevens (1992), in her review of 19 studies on the health care experiences of lesbians and bisexual women, reported that many delayed seeking treatment because of fear or discomfort with their health care providers.

∞ NOTE

1. It is important to note that many lesbians and bisexual women have sex with men and therefore need contraceptive and family planning services.

2

Communication

---&---

Cindy and Christine

Cindy and Christine were in an intimate and sexual relationship for more than 40 years. However, neither was comfortable with the terms that had become popular to describe female-female relationships; they referred to each other as "roommates." During Cindy's yearly physical exam, her provider asked her how her "lover" was doing. Cindy turned away and did not return the next year for her annual physical or mammogram.

Joanne

Joanne, after much resistance, made an appointment for a Pap smear. As she filled out the intake forms, her discomfort and distrust were immediately heightened. She was asked to indicate her marital status by choosing from one of the following categories: married, single, divorced, separated, or widowed—none of which described her 11-year monogamous relationship with her female partner. She was then asked to indicate her "spouse's" name and occupation. Anxious about the confidentiality of her medical records and her providers' responses, she left both questions blank. By the time she saw the gynecologist, she found it very difficult to relax or discuss her health.

*Once in the office, her discomfort was reinforced when her provider
asked, "Are you sexually active?" After she told him she was, he continued, "What method of birth control do you use?" Joanne stammered, "I
don't use birth control." The doctor proceeded to lecture her on the
traumas of unplanned pregnancies, further reinforcing Joanne's discomfort and mistrust.*

——————— ℮ ———————

*I*n both of these cases, the providers were doing
what they believed they should to provide
their patients with optimal care. Yet, their in-
sensitivity about the importance of the terminology the patients preferred created barriers to providing a positive relationship with their
patients. Although well-intentioned, Cindy's provider was unaware of
how uncomfortable the term *lover* made her feel. Had he used the
terminology that she had used—*roommate*—communication would
have been facilitated rather than blocked.

Joanne, from the very beginning of her appointment, was made to
feel uneasy. Where she should have felt encouraged for having a Pap
smear, she felt stress and anger. Her provider's assumptions about the
gender of her sexual partners kept her from opening up regarding the
nature of her sexual activity. He could not obtain accurate information
about her sexual risks or give her counseling on appropriate types of
protection. It is unlikely that Joanne will return for further preventive
care. A heightened sensitivity to language could have created a much
friendlier and more positive health care environment for both women.

✄ COMMUNICATION BETWEEN PATIENTS
AND PROVIDERS

Along with diagnosing and treating physical symptoms, health
professionals are an important source of information and counseling.
They reinforce healthy behaviors, influence lifestyle changes, and are

often the gateway for their patients' access to additional sources of health information and care. In addition, they influence other areas of their patients' lives, such as determining whether their patients are able to work, when they should be entitled to disability payments, and sometimes, as in the case of mental health providers, testifying as to whether a woman is fit to parent.

As with all relationships, communication is a key factor to successful patient-provider relationships. Researchers analyzing tape recordings of hundreds of doctor-patient communications have found that the way the provider communicates is closely correlated with both provider and patient satisfaction, the willingness of the patients to return to their provider, and the patients' compliance with medical advice. They have also found direct evidence that communication influences health outcomes (Roter & Hall, 1992). Specifically, Hall and her colleagues found in their analysis of dozens of research studies analyzing recordings of provider-patient interactions, that the more information a provider gave, the more satisfied patients were with their visits and the greater their compliance with medical advice. In much the same way, the more the provider attempted to include the patient in treatment decisions, the more satisfied the patients were and the more likely they were to remember the information that was exchanged. In addition, the more social conversation during the visit, the more satisfied the patients were with their care.

Although detailed analyses of provider-patient interactions have not been conducted specifically with lesbians and bisexual women and their providers, in a study of 133 lesbians in a Northern California county it was observed that the women who were open about their sexual orientation with their provider were more satisfied with their care and used preventive care more regularly than women who did not disclose their sexual orientation (Gruskin, 1995).

Provider-patient relationships are often especially strained for lesbian and bisexual patients. Communication difficulties are a primary cause of negative relationships with providers and may be one of the reasons that lesbians are less likely to receive regular care than their heterosexual counterparts (O'Hanlan, 1995). In fact, one of the most common complaints lesbians and bisexual women have about their providers is the way the provider attempts to elicit information from them, especially as it relates to their relationships or their sexuality.

Research conducted by sociologist Howard Waitzkin (1991) illuminates the types of difficulties that lesbians and bisexual women have with their providers. He found, in detailed analyses of the language used by providers when interacting with their patients, that providers reinforce societal norms, especially with reference to gender roles. Given that providers' attitudes about homosexuality generally reflect the negative attitudes dominating the mainstream, it is not surprising that many would reinforce society's heterosexual ideals. And since patients are often sensitive to the reactions of their health providers, it follows that expressions of these negative attitudes can make lesbians and bisexual women uncomfortable.

The following are examples of sequences of questions that make it difficult for lesbians and bisexual women to be open about their relationships with women, followed by alternative neutral language. Notice how the gender-neutral alternatives could facilitate communication.

> **Gender specific:** *Are you married?*
>
> **Gender neutral:** *Are you in a committed relationship? Or, Is there someone you would like to include in discussions about your treatment?*
>
> **Gender specific:** *Would you like to bring your husband or boyfriend to your next visit with you?*
>
> **Gender neutral:** *Is there anyone you would like to bring with you to your next appointment?*
>
> **Gender specific:** *You should probably have your boyfriend or husband come in to be assessed for Herpes as well. You can have him contact me to set up an appointment.*
>
> **Gender neutral:** *Is there someone with whom you have been sexually active recently? Is this person a male or female? You should probably have him or her come in to be assessed for Herpes as well.*

Gender neutral language allows the patient to disclose the gender of her partner and to provide appropriate information on her own terms, without having to fight, resist, or deny her providers' assumptions. The result is an atmosphere of greater trust and more openness.

USING APPROPRIATE LANGUAGE AND TERMINOLOGY

Language is communication. For lesbian and bisexual women language is even more critical because of the complexity of the ways they construct their personal relationships and lives. Like any other group of patients, lesbians and bisexual women share some commonalties, but there is also great diversity in the way they view their experiences and their identity. Understanding of and sensitivity to language and terminology are thus essential to effective communication between providers and patients. The following discussions of terminology will help illustrate key concepts that affect interactions with lesbian and bisexual women.

Gender and Sexuality

As infants, we are assigned to a socially constructed *gender* based on our biological sex. If we have an "adequate" penis, we are a boy, and if we have a vagina, we are a girl. In "ambiguous" cases (intersexuality), the doctor typically assigns a gender (to assist with this decision chromosome tests are available) and surgically alters the genitalia to match.[1] Along with the *gender assignment* comes a wide range of *gender expectations* such as physical manifestations (clothing, hair length, makeup), mannerisms (the appropriate way to walk or stand, levels of aggression, interactions with members of the same and opposite genders), and aspirations (career, family).

Sexual identity refers to the individual's own perception of the gender of the people to whom she is sexually attracted or with whom she has sexual relationships. *Sexual preference* implies that sexual attractions are chosen, while *sexual orientation* implies that these attractions are innate and therefore beyond the individual's control.

In a simple framework, *heterosexuals* are attracted to and have sexual and intimate relationships with members of the opposite sex, while *homosexuals* are attracted to and are sexual with members of the same sex, and *bisexuals* are drawn to both the same and opposite sex.

Heterosexuals are frequently called *straight,* although this term is often rejected by lesbians and bisexual women because it implies that nonheterosexuals are crooked or not normal. Other words used by lesbians and bisexual women for heterosexuals include *hets, heteros,* or the more derogatory term *breeders*. Lesbians and bisexual women often reject the term *homosexual*, because it emphasizes sexuality and because it is a clinical term that has been used by the dominant culture to refer to a psychological pathology. Homosexual women often prefer the terms *lesbian* or *gay*. Gay however, because it is the term used for men, can make lesbians feel invisible. Some lesbians and bisexual women (as well as other feminists) use the terms *woman-identified-woman* or *woman-loving woman*. Woman or women may be spelled *womyn, womon,* or *wimmin* by those who would prefer a term that does not include "men" or "man."

Most bisexual women use the terms *bisexual* or *bi*, although some women who have relationships with both men and women identify as lesbians, especially around their lesbian friends. Until very recently, bisexuals were rejected by both lesbians and heterosexuals, making this identity difficult to live with.

Each of the terms used to describe people who have same-gendered relationships is charged both politically and socially. When a woman accepts these identities, or if she chooses not to accept them but is identified by others as exhibiting the behaviors, she becomes a member of a *sexual minority* that most societies consider immoral, sick, and/or illegal.

Some women may not identify with these communities because they feel that they represent primarily white middle to upper class people, or because they do not agree with the political ideology that lesbians and bisexual women should be visible rather than assimilating into mainstream society. Such women may reject all of the preceding terminology. Instead, they may avoid using any language that describes their attractions and relationships with people of the same sex, or they may use the heterosexual terms accepted by their culture or society at large.

This may be especially true for older women and women of color. Sometimes, to include women who do not identify as lesbian, but who have relationships with women, the term *women who have sex with women* (WSW) is used by health professionals. This term focuses on behavior instead of, or in addition to, the other terms identified above.

Other terms describing sexual minorities are even more loaded and controversial. Although some lesbians and bisexual women use the term *dyke* to describe themselves and each other, especially when referring to activists and women who reject mainstream values, the term can have negative connotations. As a rule of thumb, health professionals should only use the term dyke with their patient when they know that it is acceptable to her.

The increasingly used term *queer* is also controversial. Many gays, lesbians, bisexuals, and transgendered people have embraced the term and use it to describe all sexual and gender minorities. Although the inclusiveness of this term is appealing and those who use it believe that "claiming" a term takes away the power from others who use it as an insult; it has negative connotations for many within these communities, especially for older members. The term *queer* also has political connotations; many of those who use it believe in an inclusive movement with freedom of sexual and gender expression rather than an emphasis on assimilation into the mainstream. The term *queer* should be used by the health care provider only with extreme caution. In fact, in some states, the term queer is an indication that a crime was a hate crime.

The term *two-spirited* is used by some Native American tribes as an inclusive term describing gender and sexual minorities. This positive term came from the idea that two-spirited people can see through both the male's and the female's eyes, making them especially powerful and spiritual.

Separatism is a concept sometimes used to describe lesbian and bisexual women who choose to spend their time in spaces without heterosexuals and/or men. They may feel that they cannot attain position and respect with men or heterosexuals around. The separatist movement was stronger in the 1970s than it is today, although there are still many women who spend some time in women-only spaces. Having women-only spaces is important because at most events, activities, and gathering places that allow both men and women, even in the gay community, men greatly outnumber women.

Gender Identity

Gender identity reflects the match between our sex at birth and the gender that we perceive ourselves to be. An individual's gender identity does not determine her sexual orientation.

Many lesbians and bisexual women identify as *butch, femme,* or *androgynous.* Butch women often have what others might consider masculine behaviors or appearances such as wearing their hair very short or wearing traditionally male clothing. Femmes may appear more

feminine by mainstream standards. *Androgynous* women do not identify as either butch or femme, choosing instead to have a more neutral
gender identity. These identities often shape relationships, especially
their sexual aspects. *Butch-femme* identities and relationships were very
common among working class women in the 1950s and 1960s, where
they structured the culture, providing women with a way to relate to
each other that fit into a heterosexual world. It may be particularly
difficult for butch women to obtain sensitive health care because they
often face discrimination for breaking gender norms. Butch or femme
women may or may not consider themselves to be transgendered.

Transsexuals are people who see themselves as having a different
gender from the sex they were born with and therefore try to live their
lives in their *preferred gender*. There are heterosexual, homosexual, and
bisexual transsexual people. For transsexuals, *sex reassignment surgery*
(SRS) is the method by which they can choose to change their primary
sexual features so that they match their gender identity. Transsexuals
may be *non-op*, that is, live their lives in their preferred gender identity
but do not plan to have SRS; *pre-op*, that is, plan to have the surgery but
have not had it; and *post-op*, namely, have had the surgery. *Female to*
Males (FTMs) are born in female bodies and transition to male bodies,
whereas *Male to Females (MTFs)* are born in male bodies and transition
to female bodies. A *transsexual woman* is an MTF whereas a *transsexual*
man is an FTM. These categories are important for health care providers
because they entail different medical, psychological, and social needs.

Transsexuals fit under the umbrella term *transgendered*, a term also
used to describe those who dress in clothing typical of the opposite
gender (*cross dresser*), but who do not feel that their gender identity does
not match their natal biological sex as transsexuals do. Transgendered
may also include people who impersonate people from the opposite
gender (*female* or *male impersonators* or *drag kings* or *drag queens*). Finally,
transgendered may also include both butch women and men who have
what others might consider strong "feminine" traits.

Negative Attitudes Toward Lesbian
and Bisexual Women

Americans use several terms to describe negative feelings and
attitudes about homosexuality. Two of the most common are *homophobia*
and *heterosexism* (see Chapter 3 for a detailed discussion).

Terms for the Relationships Between Lesbian and Bisexual Women

Lesbians and bisexual women have yet to find a universal term to describe their female partners. Some people use terms that are common for heterosexual relationships such as *spouse, significant other,* or *wife.* However, others are uncomfortable with terms that are understood primarily in a heterosexual context. The term *lover* is often used, but some women are uncomfortable with the sexual emphasis. The term *partner* is also widely accepted, but can be confused with a business partner. Variations of partner such as *life partner* or *domestic partner* help clarify the nature of the relationship.

Domestic partner is used for legal or policy purposes for both same-gendered and opposite-gendered relationships for individuals who have chosen not to or are unable to get married. Health care and other benefits are sometimes available for domestic partners. Some women in same-sex relationships prefer to use the term *roommates* or avoid using any of these terms—these women typically do not identify as lesbians.

Lesbians, gays, and bisexuals have their own ways of celebrating their commitment to each other, since in most places, traditional marriages are illegal. *Commitment ceremonies* take a wide variety of formats and meanings. Sometimes same-gendered couples exchange rings and vows, while other couples have chosen alternate ways of validating their relationships.

It is generally safe for health professionals to use the terminology that the individual uses. If she introduces her "lover," then it is appropriate to refer to her the same way. The terms *partner* or *significant other* are typically accepted. Throughout this book the term *partner* will be used. Similarly, if a woman introduces her *roommate,* it is an indication that she is comfortable with this term. If you are unsure, you can always ask the individual which terms she prefers, but it is important to avoid forcing her to use terminology that makes her uncomfortable.

Terms for Acknowledgment and Disclosure of Sexual Identity

Often people who are unwilling or unable to disclose their sexual orientation are said to be *closeted* or *in the closet*. In contrast, when a person identifies herself or is identified by others as a lesbian or bisexual person, then she is *out (of the closet)*. These terms have also been used to describe a person's disclosure of her sexual behavior (i.e., people can choose to be "out" about sadomasochistic sexual activity or keep this part of their lives closeted).

The continuous and complex process by which people disclose their sexual orientation to themselves and to others is called *coming out* or, more formally, *sexual identity formation* (see Chapter 4 for a detailed discussion). When a person *comes out to herself* it usually means she has acknowledged her same-gendered feelings and has begun to think of herself as a lesbian or a bisexual woman.

Outing is a term used when someone else discloses an individual's sexual orientation either by accident or on purpose. There is much controversy over outing well-known political leaders or celebrities. Simply, those who "out" others believe that by remaining in the closet, they harm the lesbian, gay, bisexual, and transgendered community at large, whereas others believe that every person, including public figures, deserves privacy. Bisexual women sometimes come out as bisexual after having already come out as lesbian when they have both same and opposite gendered attractions or relationships.

Community and Culture

Perhaps the most complex concepts are *community* and *culture*. Community is often used by the mainstream to describe either a group of people living in the same geographic location or people who are connected by other characteristics or beliefs such as ethnic, racial, or religious communities. Community is often associated with a sense of cohesion.

Similarly, lesbians, gays, bisexuals, and transgendered people use *community* to describe people who share their identity. However, it is not that simple. The diversity of people within this "community" and the geographic dispersion makes the use of this singular term controversial. Lesbians and bisexual women experience tremendous variation in their attachment to and identification with the "gay community." It is important, therefore, for health providers not to make any assumptions about the likelihood of a woman's feelings of membership in the lesbian and bisexual women's community.

Women of color who are lesbian and bisexual activists, who feel underrepresented by the primarily white visible gay community, as well as other people who do not feel the cohesiveness they associate with community use the plural form, *communities* or sometimes attach specific classifiers (i.e., African American lesbian community).

Culture, on the other hand, is more descriptive of values, common experiences, and feelings that have been produced by this community. Although there is a wealth of information about a very rich gay, lesbian, bisexual, and transgendered culture; including literature, art, historical events, organizations, music, etc., the most visible aspects pertain to the experiences of white men.

Symbols and Signifiers of Lesbians and Bisexual Women

Along with terminology, it is helpful to become familiar with the symbols that lesbians, gays, bisexuals, and transgendered people use to identify themselves to the mainstream or to each other. These symbols are particularly important as signals when people feel unable to come out in general, but want to let other lesbian, bisexual, gay, and transgendered people know about their identity.

Perhaps the most popular and inclusive symbols are the rainbow and the inverted pink triangle. Although the rainbow flag is generally a positive symbol for lesbians, gays, bisexuals, and transgendered people, the inverted pink triangle (used to identify male homosexuals) or the inverted black triangle (used to signify lesbians and other "abnormal" women) in Hitler's concentration camps, have negative historical connotations.

The lambda is another symbol used to identify both men and women in the lesbian, gay, bisexual, and transgendered communities. Symbols used for women only include the Labrys (a two-sided ax), a double women's sign for lesbians, and a modified version for bisexuals that includes the upward arrow of the symbol for a male. Red ribbons signify victims, survivors, and those who empathize with the HIV/AIDS crisis among both gays and non-gays. The blue and black striped flag with a heart in the left-hand corner is the symbol for the sadomasochistic or leather community.

All of these symbols and terms may be displayed on clothing, pins, buildings, jewelry, flyers, businesses, or as part of a logo, identifying either gay, lesbian, bisexual, or transgendered people to each other or to others who want to welcome this community. Displaying these symbols and logos in offices and clinics is a way to indicate to the lesbian and bisexual women's community that there are lesbian, gay or bisexual people employed there and that they are welcome.

Activities and Events Important to Lesbian and Bisexual Women

In any culture or community, certain events are remembered and commemorated. Gay men, lesbians, bisexuals, and transgendered people are no exception. Perhaps the best known is the Stonewall Rebellion, when a group of gay, lesbian, bisexual, and transgendered people fought back against one of the many police raids of a gay bar, the Stonewall Inn in New York City on June 25, 1969. This event has been celebrated internationally ever since, with special anniversary marches and gay pride celebrations. These events can be powerful, especially for people who have little connection with the lesbian, gay, bisexual, and transgendered communities, or who have recently come out. The entire month of June is often one of celebration and visibility for the lesbian, gay, bisexual, and transgendered communities.

Many lesbians and bisexual women gather at women's music festivals, where thousands of women camp together sharing music, educational seminars, social events, and discussing politics. Finally, on October 9th, gays, lesbians, bisexuals, and transgendered people come together on *national coming out day.* Many people use the occasion to disclose their sexual or gender identity in general or with specific people on a day when they know they will receive encouragement and community support. It is a day of rallies, protests, and celebrations for many.

In addition to learning the terminology that lesbian and bisexual women are likely to use to describe themselves, their relationships, and their lives, it is important to look in more depth at sexuality and gender identity. Although knowing the right terms and using them appropriately can improve communication between health care providers and their lesbian and bisexual women patients, it is even more essential to have a conceptual framework within which to understand behavior and identity. Most models and theories from the past have been neither adequate nor accurate, focusing as they have on exclusive and definitive categories that may fail to clarify either the individual's experiences or society's interpretations. Rather, it is important to see sexuality as a continuum with various components, including the way the individual sees herself, the way she perceives herself to be viewed by others, and her behavior.

◁ A NEW MODEL OF SEXUALITY AND GENDER IDENTITY

——————— ℮ ———————

Nancy

Nancy went to her gynecologist with complaints of chronic yeast infections a few months after entering into her first relationship with a woman. In the beginning of her exam, Nancy told her provider that she was excited about her plans to attend the gay pride celebration the following weekend. Her provider assumed from this and from Nancy's lesbian rights T-shirt that Nancy was a lesbian and therefore at low risk for HIV/AIDS. She treated the yeast infection without inquiring about Nancy's sexual behavior and other risks for HIV/AIDS, and did not offer her information on HIV testing.

Nancy returned and saw a different gynecological provider a few months later, with continued complaints of a chronic yeast infection. This provider, who was more sensitive to the complexity of sexuality, asked Nancy how many sexual partners she had had in the last 5 years, their gender, and whether she thought they might have been at risk for HIV. He further inquired about her sexual behavior and the protection she used. He discovered that, although Nancy identified as a lesbian, she had had an unprotected relationship with an IV-drug-using man within the past 2 years. He also learned that Nancy and her current partner both perceived that, since they were lesbians, they were at low risk for HIV. Therefore, they were not using dental dams or other forms of protection even though her partner had had multiple relationships over the past several years. Nancy's gynecologist advised her to have an HIV test and to use protection when having sex with both men and with women.

——————— ℮ ———————

Health professionals tend to simplify sexuality in order to make it manageable and to spare themselves and their patients the discomfort of asking personal questions. However, the assumptions that health professionals make by trying to simplify these issues can impede their ability to fully understand their patients. Nancy's first provider made assumptions about her behavior based on clues she had picked up about Nancy's identity rather than on the basis of specific, targeted questions. On the other hand, Nancy's second provider, who probed further with specific, relevant questions, made more appropriate clinical decisions.

Gender and sexuality include tremendously complex issues: definitions of sexuality; the implications of these identities inside and outside the lesbian, gay, bisexual, and transgendered communities; the diversity of behaviors of the people identifying with each label; and the taboos in many cultures about speaking openly about sexuality. For some women, a simple model of sexuality describes them quite well, for others it is not as simple.

———————— e ————————

Stephanie

Stephanie's upper-middle class, Jewish family lives in the suburbs of New York City. Stephanie first questioned her sexual orientation in her freshman year of college when she fell in love with her roommate. From that point on, whenever Stephanie used medical services, she identified herself as a lesbian and spoke freely about her intimate partner. In fact, she and her partner often used the same providers, and when appropriate, were involved in each others' treatment.

Cindy

Cindy, at the age of 20 came out to her family and friends as a lesbian. However, since then, she has had monogamous relationships with both men and women and can imagine being in a long-term relationship with either a man or a woman. When asked about her sexual orientation, she usually answers, "I love people."

———————— e ————————

Lesbian or bisexual identity is personal, social, political, and cultural, shaping the way a woman sees the world and impacting her social networks, her relationships, and her political ideology. When a woman identifies as a lesbian or bisexual woman, on the one hand, she becomes a member of a minority considered immoral, illegal, and/or sick by many in mainstream society. She faces discomfort, discrimination, and even verbal and physical assault by those who discover and disapprove of her identity. Uneducated people often assume that she fits the mythical stereotype of lesbians as "man-haters" or that she has chosen to be with women because she "could not find a man." On the other hand, that same woman becomes part of a group that offers a wealth of support, organizations, culture, and events that can make her feel included and accepted to whatever extent she wishes. For example, when traveling, lesbians and bisexual women can locate bookstores, bed and breakfast inns, and bars where they know they will feel at home and be accepted.

Identifying as a lesbian for many women is a political statement that reinforces the importance of women's equality and ability to survive without sexual intimacy with men. Women may identify as lesbian prior to having sexual relationships with women, when they are abstinent, or even when having sexual relationships with men.

A bisexual identity is also tremendously complex. Although bisexual women have recently begun to feel more supported and accepted by a growing bisexual community and the lesbian and gay community, bisexuality is still often not accepted or respected by either heterosexuals or homosexuals. Many bisexuals therefore feel that they must hide their identity. But, like a lesbian identity, a bisexual identity is not necessarily dictated by the gender of the person with whom the woman is sexual and intimate. For example, many women who are in long-term, monogamous relationships with women still acknowledge their attraction to men and, if asked, say that they are bisexual.

Theorists, researchers, and activists have proposed several models for assessing sexual identity. Perhaps the best known, the Kinsey Scale, was developed by Alfred Kinsey and his colleagues in the mid 1950s. His six-point scale ranges from 0 (*exclusively heterosexual*) to 6 (*exclusively homosexual*) with bisexual in the middle (3). This continuum expands the number of categories of sexual orientation from the two categories, homosexual and heterosexual, to seven (Blumenfeld, 1988). Kinsey's Scale did not, however, differentiate among the many components of sexuality, such as identity and behavior. Similar scales are used to assess individuals on more than one dimension; including sexual behavior, fantasies, long-term relationships, and sexual feelings. Also inherent in the design of these scales is a balance between heterosexuality and homosexuality for each individual (i.e., if you are more heterosexual, you are less homosexual).

Another way to understand sexual orientation is parallel dimensions in multiple domains (Garnets, Hancock, Cochran, Goodchilds, & Peplau, 1991). Rather than placing homosexual and heterosexual as opposite extremes on one continuum, this model proposes that there are many dimensions (e.g., sexual attractions, current sexual behavior, past behavior, fantasies, etc.) where an individual can rate as same-gendered and opposite-gendered.

An illustrative metaphor of a stereo equalizer can be used for this parallel dimensional model. On many stereo equalizers, there are treble and bass adjustments for several sets of speakers. One adjustment is not contingent upon the other adjustments. For example, you can adjust for high bass and high treble, low bass and low treble, or high bass and low treble for each speaker, individually. In much the same way, an individual can be strongly sexually attracted to women *and* to men; to one gender or the other, or to neither gender. An attraction to one gender does not preclude or infer an attraction to the other gender.

To continue the stereo equalizer analogy, each set of speakers can represent a different dimension of sexuality. Once again, an adjustment on one set of "speakers" does not determine a particular adjustment on another set. An individual can have a strong lesbian identity (set 1), be attracted to both men and women (set 2), and engage in sexual relationships only with women (set 3). Although the settings of the various sets do not directly affect each other, together they produce a particular experience. A woman who identifies as a lesbian and has sexual relationships with women has different experiences from a woman who identifies as a lesbian and has sexual relationships with both men and women and vice versa. The model includes both current and past behavior.

The equalizer model is particularly useful to health professionals because it allows them to minimize assumptions, while collecting detailed and specific information about their patients. Within this framework, providers can identify the dimensions that are relevant (i.e., past, current, and future sexual behavior; identity; and support from the lesbian, gay, and bisexual community) and ask their patients direct questions about their relationships both with women and men.

Examples may help. Here is a list of questions with the responses that might describe three women, who when asked their sexual orientation, might give the same response, but when situated in a more complex framework are very different.

	Allison	*Carry*	*Tammy*
Cognitive Sexual Orientation			
Fantasies with women	*strong*	*strong*	*strong*
Fantasies with men	*strong*	*weak*	*none*
Sexual Behavior			
Current sexual behavior with men	*none*	*about 4/year*	*none*
Current sexual behavior with women	*bi-weekly*	*weekly*	*weekly*
Past sexual behavior with men	*none*	*12 partners*	*none*
Past sexual relationship with women	*5 partners*	*8 partners*	*7 partners*
Self-Identity			
Current lesbian self-identity	*strong*	*strong*	*strong*
Current heterosexual self-identity	*none*	*none*	*none*
Current bisexual self-identity	*none*	*weak*	*none*
Female gender identity	*strong*	*strong*	*strong*
Male gender identity	*none*	*none*	*none*
Butch/Femme identity	*butch*	*androgynous*	*femme*
Identity with Lesbian/Bi/Trans Community			
Participates in community	*weekly*	*weekly*	*monthly*
Out About Sexual Identity/Orientation			
Family	*all*	*most*	*disowned*
Friends	*all*	*all*	*all*
Work	*all*	*none*	*none*
Perceived Labeling by Others			
She thinks others see her as heterosexual	*none*	*some*	*some*
She thinks others see her as lesbian	*all*	*most*	*some*
She thinks others see her as bisexual	*none*	*some*	*none*
Sees herself having future w/man	*none*	*none*	*none*
Sees herself having future w/woman	*strong*	*strong*	*strong*
Others see her as female	*some*	*most*	*some*
Others see her as male	*some*	*some*	*some*

Others see her as transsexual	some	none	some
Sex			
Natal female genitalia	yes	yes	no
Current secondary female sex characteristics	yes	yes	yes

If the health professional asked any of these women what their sexual orientation was, they would all answer "lesbian." Many providers would assume from this that all three women have sexual relationships only with women and therefore not offer them birth control counseling or STD protection. However, if they understood the complexity of sexuality and asked more specific questions, they would find out that Carry, although identifying as a lesbian, had had sexual relationships with men in the past and continued to do so occasionally, putting her at risk for sexually transmitted diseases and pregnancy. Therefore, STD and pregnancy counseling would be appropriate. If they asked further about their lives, they would find out that Allison, being butch in her identity and her demeanor, might be at high risk for discrimination because of her physical appearance, regardless of whether she chose to reveal her sexual identity. They would also learn that Carry was closeted with her family and at work and might be dealing with stress, and that it is crucial to protect her confidentiality so that her workplace does not find out about her sexual orientation through her medical records. Similarly, Tammy's stress will most likely be high around her transition from male to female and when she is "clocked" (others guess that she is not a natal female) and that she does not have family support. Finally, by inquiring about their participation in the lesbian and bisexual women's community, the provider has learned that if necessary and available, treatment specifically designed for lesbian and bisexual women (i.e., drug or alcohol treatment or mental health treatment) might be appropriate, and that they have both their supports and negative behaviors reinforced by this community.

◅ IMPLICATIONS FOR HEALTH PROFESSIONALS

✦ Nothing can be assumed about a person's behavior based solely on the terms that they use to describe themselves or how they

answer questions about their identity. Many women who identify as lesbians have had or will continue to have sexual relationships with men. Similarly, we cannot assume that a person will
have a particular identity based on the way in which she describes her behavior. Rather, specific and direct questions can
elicit accurate and relevant information.

✦ Being aware of the sociocultural implications of same-sex sexual
behavior and identification can be useful in increasing sensitivity
when inquiring about the sexuality and related health issues of
patients. Patients' trust can be gained by acknowledging how
difficult it can be to disclose one's sexual orientation, especially
in a health care environment; by asking gender neutral questions
so that patients can disclose same-sex sexual activity without
having to correct assumptions; and by letting patients know the
steps that will be taken to protect their confidentiality.

✦ Health care professionals should consider what information they
believe to be relevant and ask specific questions about sexuality
and identity. For example, if a woman presents vaginal symptoms, then to diagnose her correctly, the health professional
should ask about her sexual behavior. But, if they want to learn
more about her life, then her sexual identity, gender identity, and
her participation in the lesbian/ bisexual women's community
are also important. Similarly, HIV/AIDS health educators will
want to understand the individual's sexual behavior so that they
can provide appropriate advice about protection and fully understand her sexual risks. In addition, understanding her identity
and her participation in the lesbian/bisexual community will
help them to understand the information that she is likely to
receive about HIV/ AIDS and the social dynamics of her life. This
information may also help the professional understand the cultural norms of her community.

✦ A therapist needs to have an in-depth understanding of an
individual's identification, the discrimination she is likely to
confront because of her identity and her behavior, her social
networks, and the communities with which she identifies.

✦ Clearly, labels such as lesbian, heterosexual, and bisexual do not
reflect the complexity of sexual orientation, nor do they give
health professionals a comprehensive understanding of their

patients' health-related behaviors or beliefs. *If in doubt, ask.* If you note your patient's discomfort with terms you use or questions you ask, acknowledge the discomfort and ask about the terms that are preferred. For example, "That term seemed to make you uncomfortable. Is there a different word you would prefer that I use?"

+ Research has demonstrated how critical communication with patients is to accurate diagnoses, patients' compliance with medical advice, effectiveness in providing health education and counseling, satisfaction with care, and, therefore, patients' health outcomes. This is especially true for women who feel they have to hide aspects of themselves from health providers to protect themselves from discomfort or discrimination. Careful attention to the communication process enhances provider relationships with lesbian and bisexual patients.

+ Lesbian and bisexual women face significant risks in disclosing their sexual orientation to their health professional if their confidentiality is not maintained. Specific indication of how their confidentiality will be protected may encourage them to be open about their sexual identity and behavior.

✑ NOTE

1. However, there are increasing numbers of health professionals and intersex advocates who believe that surgery on children, unless medically necessary, is harmful to the child.

3

Homophobia and Heterosexism

―――――――ℰ―――――――

Louise

At the age of 17, Louise went to Dr. Sanders, one of the few doctors in her rural farming community, with the symptoms of a vaginal infection. When the doctor asked her if she had been sexual with boys, Louise burst into tears and ran from the room. Louise's mother, Edna, confided to Dr. Sanders that she had found Louise and her best friend, Carla, sleeping in each others' arms and that she found a book on lesbians in her room. Edna clearly was very upset.

Dr. Sanders suggested that Edna find Louise a counselor and/or talk to their minister. Although the counselor Edna chose believed that he could change Louise's sexual orientation with behavior modification, he only made Louise feel worse about herself. Louise and Carla continued to see each other behind their parents' backs. They did not meet any other lesbians until they attended community college in a small city where they continued their relationship.

Inez and Sandra

Inez and Sandra were walking through the streets of New York after having spent the evening dancing at their favorite nightclub. They heard a group of boys come up behind them hissing "dyke" and "bitch" under their breath. They tried to get away but the boys moved closer, their epithets becoming louder and clearer. "Think you're a f—ing man? I'll teach you what a man is." They circled the two women, drawing closer and closer until they eventually attacked. They gang raped and beat both women and left them unconscious. The attack left Inez with chronic back problems and Sandra severely depressed for several months after the incident.

Jan

When Jan, a transsexual lesbian, went to an emergency room to receive care for the wounds she received as a result of homophobic violence, she overheard the doctor telling the nurse to take care of the "faggot." Jan left the emergency room before she could be treated.

Mishi

Mishi, a second generation Chinese woman, was hospitalized after a suicide attempt. During her stay, she told her doctor that she tried to kill herself because she did not want to stop seeing Nancy, her partner, but she could not continue disgracing her family.

———————— ☙ ————————

*O*n American society, heterosexuality is the only acceptable form of sexuality. As recently as 1994, 62% of Americans surveyed by the National Research Center believed that adult homosexual relations were "always wrong." Similarly, the 1992 Gallop Poll results indicated that only 38% of Americans surveyed believed that homosexuality was an "acceptable lifestyle" (Herek, 1997).

Straying from the heterosexual ideal can result in the lesbian or bisexual woman being arrested, beaten, killed or verbally harassed, losing employment or housing, losing the support of family and other loved ones, or losing her children. She often internalizes negative feelings about homosexuality, resulting in self-destructive behavior such as alcohol use, depression, and even suicide. While some lesbians and bisexual women choose whether or not to disclose their sexual orientation, others overtly fit the stereotypes and people assume that they are lesbian.

The counselor that Louise saw thought it would be better to try to change her sexual orientation than to help her learn to accept it. The hate violence that Inez and Sandra (and over 2,212 others in 1995) (National Coalition of Anti-Violence Programs, 1996) experienced affected them not only physically, but emotionally by taking away their sense of security and safety. When Jan most needed support and care, she was victimized again both emotionally and physically, directly interfering with the care that she received. Mishi, feeling that she had no viable options, attempted to end her life.

✑ TERMS AND DEFINITIONS

Homophobia, the most commonly used term describing anti-gay feelings, means literally, fear of the same; in this case, fear of same-gendered sexuality. However, the term homophobia is also commonly used to mean hatred toward homosexuals. This term may be deceiving, however, because it implies that fear is the cause of anti-gay feelings. For many people homophobia does not result solely from the fear of homosexuality, but rather a host of hypothesized reasons such as a need to be a part of a group or the need to reinforce one's values (Herek, 1992).

Heterosexism, or the belief that heterosexuality is the only acceptable form of sexuality, is another term often used synonymously with homophobia. It is useful to differentiate between heterosexism and homophobia. In one framework, homophobia involves direct and strong anti-gay feelings often associated with some type of action, while heterosexism is a lack of acknowledgment of the existence of homosexuals or the assumption that all people are heterosexual. Heterosexism may not be intentional, whereas homophobia, according to these definitions, is intentional. Both occur among individuals and groups and at the institutional level. (See Table 3.1.)

TABLE 3.1 External and Internal Homophobia and Heterosexism

	External	
	Homophobia	*Heterosexism*
Individual	A health care provider repeats an anti-lesbian joke in front of a patient.	During her first examination, a health care provider confronts a lesbian client for not using birth control, assuming that she has sex with men.
	A therapist insists that his patient try reparative therapy to change her sexual orientation.	A provider assumes that the domestic abuse that her patient has been undergoing is from a male, when in fact the woman is being abused by a woman.
Group	A group of teenagers assault a classmate after they find out that she is bisexual.	A group of little girls refuse to play house with two mothers, even though one of the little girls is being raised by two lesbians.
	A group of therapists refuse to display literature that a lesbian counseling organization has sent them on a new group for lesbians because they think that it will negatively affect the rest of their patients.	A group of doctors only display representations of heterosexual couples in their health education materials.
Institutional	A medical school refuses to accept students who indicate on their application that they are lesbian, gay, or bisexual.	A professional organization does not include sexual orientation in their discrimination clause.
	A large company, after consideration, on moral grounds, refuses to allow domestic partnership benefits for same-sex relationships	A large company has never considered allowing domestic partnership benefits for same-sex relationships.
Society	A sodomy statute specifically indicates that homosexual activity will be illegal in that state.	Marriage is assumed to be between a man and a woman.

TABLE 3.1 Continued

	Internal	
	Homophobia	*Heterosexism*
Individual	A young adult, after her first sexual activity with a woman, attempts suicide because she cannot live her life as a lesbian.	A lesbian does not even think about mentioning her same-sex relationship when she is being examined for a vaginal infection.
Group	A lesbian couple, both of whom really want children, decide not to have them because they do not believe that lesbians should have children.	A female couple never consider that they can have children because they are lesbians.
	A research team consisting of ex-gays seeks ways to prove that homosexuality is immoral.	A research team composed primarily of gay and lesbian researchers compares the sexual orientation of grown children of gays and lesbians to those of heterosexuals with the understanding that it is better to have heterosexual children.
Institutional	A group of ex-gays spend years in treatment trying to rid themselves of their homosexuality.	A lesbian and gay organization names their organization without the words gay and lesbian in their title.

HYPOTHESIZED CAUSES OF HOMOPHOBIA AND HETEROSEXISM

Providers are likely to confront negative attitudes about homosexuality and bisexuality as their lesbian and bisexual patients try to cope with discriminatory situations, as they witness homophobia and heterosexism by their patients and colleagues, and as they see the ways sexual minorities are treated throughout society. Providers may be asked by patients to explain where these negative feelings may be coming from or they may try to understand on their own. Gregory Herek (1992) has proposed a framework for thinking about the causes of negative attitudes toward homosexuals grounded in his own research. His work is based on the concept of psychological functionalism—the assumption that beliefs and attitudes serve a psychological function for the individual. Table 3.2, taken directly from *Hate Crimes*, a book that he co-edited, summarizes his ideas (Herek, 1992, p. 157).

Providers may also be in a position to be able to advocate for lesbian or bisexual patients or colleagues—understanding potential causes for responses can help in trying to change attitudes. For example, if negative attitudes toward lesbians and bisexual women stem from an individual's values, (i.e., I am religious; my religion is against homosexuality; therefore, in order to strengthen my affiliation with my religion, I must actively oppose homosexuality and bisexuality), pointing out other values that being actively discriminatory confronts may be a helpful technique (i.e., love thy neighbor).

EXTERNAL HOMOPHOBIA: RISKS AND IMPLICATIONS

Hate Violence

One of the most insidious threats against the physical and emotional health of lesbians and bisexual women, and the most concrete manifestation of homophobia, is hate violence. In 1994 alone, 2,212 cases of homophobic hate violence were reported in the eleven states which were part of the national tracking program, and although the number of reported hate crimes is decreasing slightly, their violent nature is increasing. The top six categories of offenses included harass-

TABLE 3.2 The Psychological Functions of Heterosexism

Name of Function	Description	Benefit to Individual
Evaluative Functions		
Experiential	Generalizes from past experiences with specific lesbians or gay men to create a coherent image of gay people in relation to one's own interests.	Makes sense of past experiences and uses them to guide behavior.
Anticipatory	Anticipates benefits or punishments expected to be received directly from lesbians or gay men.	In absence of direct experience with gay men or lesbians, plans future behavior to maximize rewards and minimize punishments.
Expressive Functions		
Social identity		
Value-expressive	Lesbians or gay men symbolize an important value conflict.	Increases self-esteem by affirming individual's view of self as a person who adheres to particular values.
Social-expressive	Lesbians or gay men symbolize the in-group or out-group.	Increases self-esteem by winning approval of others whose opinion is valued; increases sense of group solidarity.
Defensive	Lesbians or gay men symbolize unacceptable part of the self.	Reduces anxiety associated with a psychological conflict by denying and externalizing the unacceptable aspect of self and then attacking it.

ment, intimidation, assault with or without a weapon, vandalism, and attempted assault with a weapon (National Coalition of Anti-Violence Programs, 1996).

These statistics represent only a small portion of the crimes, given that many people who are victims of homophobic hate violence live in states without tracking programs or do not report the violence. Assessing the scope of the problem in a different way, Beatrice Von Schulthess (1992) found that the vast majority of the women in her survey of 400 primarily white lesbians recruited from the lesbian and bisexual women's community in San Francisco had experienced some form of anti-lesbian violence.

Hate violence has been defined as "defamation, intimidation, assault, murder, vandalism, and other abuse" by Gregory Herek and Keven Berrill (1992, p. 19), the authors of a groundbreaking book on homophobic hate. A homophobic hate crime is hate violence that is (a) legally considered a crime in the state in which it is committed and (b) can be proven to be motivated by hatred against homosexuals (e.g., by anti-gay language used during the crime or when anti-gay graffiti is left at the scene of the crime; crimes committed during lesbian, gay, bisexual, transgender celebrations; or crimes directed at lesbian, gay, bisexual, transgender organizations).

Hate violence reflects society's negative feelings about homosexuality and may increase the survivor's own insecurities or ambiguities about her sexual orientation. For lesbians and bisexual women, hate violence adds to the vulnerability that they face as females. Lesbians and bisexual women of color, and those of other minority groups may face both homophobic and other types of hate violence simultaneously.

Violence aimed at youths is particularly alarming. Young women do not have control over their lives in the ways that adults do, especially if the violence is coming from their own families or their schools. Many young lesbians and bisexual women feel compelled to leave their homes to escape violence and discrimination because of their sexual orientation or the way in which they express their gender. Five hundred records of the youth served by the Hetrick-Martin Institute, a community-based social service agency for primarily ethnic and racial minority lesbian and gay youth in New York City, revealed that these young people had been the victims of extraordinarily high levels of violence. A total of 40% of these youth reported violent physical attacks, 46% of which were gay-related. Of the gay-related physical assaults, 61% occurred in the family. Forty-four percent of the lesbians who experienced violent assaults attempted to kill themselves. Perpetrators of hate violence include not only organized groups such as skinheads and gangs of young men, but also teachers, police, and perhaps most disturbing, family members (Hunter, 1992).

Hate violence can result in a number of physical and emotional problems, perhaps the most common of which is acute and/or recurring Post-Traumatic Stress Syndrome; including problems sleeping, high levels of anxiety, inability to trust others, depression, and a loss of trust in self. The victim may respond to the trauma by abusing alcohol, drugs and tobacco, over or under-eating, or by attempting (or completing) suicide. Added to the trauma of being the victim of hate violence, women who are perceived to be lesbian or bisexual can undergo additional trauma when they attempt to report the crime to the police or to receive care and support from health care providers. In addition, a woman who chooses to report the hate violence or receive help for injuries or mental stress, may be compromising her confidentiality, resulting in further discrimination.

Hate violence not only affects the physical and emotional well-being of the individual victim, but it also creates an atmosphere of caution and fear within lesbian and bisexual communities. Homophobic hate violence is not limited to lesbians, gays, bisexual, and transgendered people who identify as such. Perpetrators target those whom they perceive to be sexual or gender minorities regardless of their orientation.

The Workplace

———————— ℮ ————————

Lori

Lori was an evaluation consultant on a public health department sponsored project designed to create a safer living environment in a lower-income community. The plan was to recruit several community activists to help assess the needs of the community and develop strategies to create change. It was very clear from the beginning of the project that the community activists were mistrustful of the health department after having been the subjects of several research projects with very little follow-up or change. It was also clear that they were weary of the evaluation component of the project.

Lori, "out" in almost all areas of her life, decided not to create any other potential barriers and kept her sexual orientation hidden from the community activists. She established a positive working relationship with the women. She had an especially powerful connection with two of the women who were from her hometown.

Several months into the project, one of the other activists asked her if she had a boyfriend. She indicated that she did not and they offered to help her "find a man." They continued these types of discussions and she felt increasingly uncomfortable working on the project. Her stress level increased dramatically, affecting her physical health as well as her relationship with her partner and with her children.

The day after a particularly stressful and heterosexist conversation about the importance of children being raised by both their mothers and their fathers, Lori was unable to get out of bed and go to work. She felt increasingly depressed and uncomfortable not only with her job situation, but with herself, for allowing herself to be forced into silence. She felt confused about when and where to disclose her sexual identity. Eventually, with the guidance of a therapist, she decided that she would not continue as the evaluation consultant during the second phase of the project.

Samantha

Samantha was in her last year of medical school and applying for internships. She ruled out most of the programs in states where lesbian sexuality was illegal, fully aware that when she and her partner planned to have children, it would be riskier in states with sodomy statutes. Within the remaining states, she thought carefully about where they might be able to find cultural events for her and her partner and eventually find support for their children. This limited her even further. Finally, she was left with only a few programs to consider and she examined the quality of the internship training offered by the programs. In each of the hospitals she visited, she decided to come out to other interns, knowing that she risked the opportunity to secure a position in these programs. However, she wanted to anticipate any potential problems prior to entering a program rather than after she had already committed herself.

Jo

Jo joined the navy right out of high school. A year before she would have been eligible for her full retirement benefits, her superior officer included in a report, that she suspected that Jo had had homosexual relations. As a bisexual, Jo had had relationships with both men and women throughout her service career. During the investigation, they found her "guilty" of homosexual behavior and she received a dishonorable discharge without her pension or her other retirement benefits.

Lesbians and bisexual women who allow others at work to know about their lesbian or bisexual identity run the risk of rejection by coworkers, discrimination from superiors, and loss of their jobs. Even if a woman is protected from discrimination by local or state laws or company policies, she is not immune to discrimination. Discrimination is extremely difficult to prove; fighting the company is a long, expensive, and emotionally draining process; and the burden of proof is on the plaintiff. In most job situations, the pressure not to disclose one's sexual orientation is very strong. But if a lesbian remains closeted, she then will have to be selective or dishonest when she talks about her life or participates in job-related activities. Whether she is open or secretive, she is likely to experience high levels of stress.

The military is the most notorious for workplace discrimination. After World War II, when the need for military personnel decreased, the policies devised by psychiatrists and medical personnel for excluding homosexuals from the armed forces were enforced. Often, when an individual was suspected of being homosexual, she was interrogated until she "confessed" and gave the names of others she knew to be homosexual. In 1982 the Department of Defense formalized a policy specifically forbidding homosexuals from serving in the armed forces. Approximately 3,740 lesbians were discharged from the military between 1980 and 1990. Although President Bill Clinton campaigned to eliminate the ban on gays in the military, he succeeded only in his "don't ask, don't tell, don't pursue policy." This policy is designed to stop the "witch hunts" for homosexuals without completely lifting the ban (Jones & Koshes, 1995).

Banning gays from the military is harmful to society as a whole, to the military, and to the lesbian/bisexual individual who wants to serve her country. The ban is the most blatant federal example of anti-homosexual discrimination. For many economically disadvantaged people, the military can serve as a refuge and a way to obtain education, job opportunities and training, and status that might not otherwise be available (Anderson & Smith, 1993). Lesbians and bisexual women who join the military fear being found out if they engage in relationships and if they participate in events in the lesbian and bisexual women's community. This can make any internalized homophobia particularly intense.

At School

Chris

Chris, a 17-year-old lesbian, was "found out" by the students and teachers in her high school. As a result, the women on her softball team began verbally harassing her and said they did not want to be in the same locker room with her. They intentionally assaulted her during practice. The softball coach asked Chris to leave the team, in spite of the fact that her senior year was critical for college recruiting. As a result, Chris became depressed, her school work suffered, and she no longer had the hope of going to a good college on a softball scholarship.

Ellen

Ellen sat quietly in her high school health class as one of the most popular teachers in the school spouted anti-gay rhetoric. She knew that she wouldn't be able to ask him about the confusing feelings that she was having. She also knew that if she and her girlfriend were "caught" that they would probably be a direct target.

For the adolescent or young adult, it is difficult to gain access to the lesbian and gay community (either through lack of resources or lack of independence from adults) and to find appropriate role models to make their orientation something they can explore without being treated as immoral or "perverted." Their peers can also be very direct and cruel in their treatment of gays and lesbians. There are continual attempts to limit financial support for institutions that provide education about or support for lesbians and gay youth. On college campuses, heterosexist professors may have a negative influence on youth who are exploring their sexual identity. But many lesbians also report professors and teachers who played important roles in their coming out process.

The Family

Lourdes

Lourdes was always masculine in appearance, treated like a tomboy and allowed to play with the boys. However, when she reached the age of 12, her parents began to worry and wanted her to become more feminine. They insisted that she wear dresses and that she spend more time with her female friends. When she was 16, Lourdes fell in love with an older friend, and during a fight with her parents about her style of dress, she told them that she was a lesbian. Her mother started crying and praying and her father told her to leave the house. She spent the next five years living on the streets until she was able to finish high school and enroll in a community college. The only health care she received while on the streets was emergency care from a youth clinic when she was treated for pneumonia.

Jennifer

Jennifer came out to her parents at 21. Their first response was extremely negative; they were completely surprised and caught off-guard. When Jennifer insisted that her father accept her sexual identity because she was his daughter, her father said, "I don't have to accept your being gay! If your brother was to turn out to be a murderer, I wouldn't have to accept him!" Having her lesbianism equated with crime served to reinforce Jennifer's own feelings of doubt and self-hatred.

Although Jennifer was lucky that her family continued to support her financially through college, they offered little emotional support and were hostile toward her partner. Later, when her parents began to come to terms with their daughter's lesbianism, they worked to rebuild their relationship.

Eventually, Jennifer's father recognized how painful his initial re-marks were and apologized to Jennifer. However, it was very difficult for Jennifer's partner to forgive Jennifer's parents and it remained a problem in their relationship.

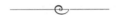

Unlike ethnic, racial, and religious minorities, most lesbians and bisexual women differ from their families in their sexual orientation. They often must cope with intensely negative reactions from within their families, especially when their families first learn of their sexual orientation. This can have direct emotional, physical, and logistical consequences. Emotionally, it is difficult for most women to be rejected by their families, especially if it is because of the person whom they love. This can result in intensified internalized homophobia for the lesbian or bisexual woman, particularly if she chooses to disclose this information early in her identity development. The disclosure of a lesbian or bisexual identity can result in verbal and physical assault, intensified control over her life (i.e., confinement, being sent to a private school, or psychiatric hospitalization), or even her being kicked out of her home.

Like the lesbian or bisexual individual, most families of the lesbian and bisexual woman go through a process by which they come to terms with their family member's sexual orientation. Although some families will never accept a member's homosexuality, many just need time to learn about and process the new information that they receive. Unfortunately, while they are coming to terms with the information, they are often unaccepting and hurtful.

The Legal System

In many states, being a lesbian is illegal because of laws that prohibit certain kinds of sexual behavior. Sodomy laws, often used as a proxy to outlaw same-sex relationships, are still on the books in almost half of the states. The legal protection that a lesbian or bisexual woman has is directly influenced by where she lives and her financial resources.

After a long, painful battle with the Virginia legal system, where there is a sodomy statute forbidding lesbian sexual activity and there is no protection for lesbians and bisexual women, Sharon Bottoms, a lesbian woman, and her female partner lost custody of Sharon's son to his biological grandmother. One of the rationales behind the decision was that the woman and her lover were breaking the law by being in a sexual relationship. Other women have lost their jobs, their housing, and access to their lovers during medical emergencies. (See Chapter 8 for a comprehensive discussion of legal issues.)

Religion

Negative religious teachings about homosexuality have created a deeply embedded core of shame and self-loathing which surfaces in a host of dysfunctional attitudes and behaviors . . . . The deep-seated guilt, shame, and fear which many gays feel manifest themselves in a variety of symptoms: low self-esteem, chronic depression, substance abuse, eating disorders, co-dependency and sexual addiction or sexual dysfunction. (Booth, 1995, p. 57-58)

Because of the religious messages which teach that women are inferior or secondary, lesbians in particular suffer a double dose of injustice. (Booth, 1995, p. 61)

Classes on religion in courses on lesbian, gay, bisexual, and transgender health and culture have always been one of the most difficult. Emotions are particularly intense during lectures, discussions, and in written responses to readings. Some students have been banished from their churches or temples because of their sexual orientation—or their families have used their own religious beliefs as reasons or excuses to reject them.

These students have been so hurt and angered by religion that they have a hard time understanding other students' responses to religion, specifically those students who either involve themselves in religious sects which accept them or those who hide their sexual identity so that they can practice their religion. For many of these students, especially those with strong ethnic affiliations, religion is a strong part of their identity and of their culture. Giving up their religion is unthinkable. They, therefore, choose to hide their sexual orientation. Some, however, have been able to find religious institutions, such as the Metropolitan Community Church and the Unitarian Universalist Church, which accept them as openly lesbian or gay, bisexual, or transsexual individuals.

Some gay and lesbian individuals have been unable to resolve the conflict between their sexual behavior and the teachings of their religions and, as in the well-known case of Bobby Griffith (Aarons, 1995), choose suicide as the only viable option. Others have chosen to become academicians focusing on studying "religiously induced homophobia."

The health professional must acknowledge the difficult position that religious individuals face and the important role of religion in sustaining homophobia. It may be important for health professionals to examine and then put aside their own personal religious beliefs about homosexuality so that their biases do not interfere with their professional role, or it may be appropriate for them to refer their lesbian and bisexual patients to other providers.

The Health Care System

Extensive research on attitudes toward homosexuals among health care providers shows a disturbing picture (Stevens, 1992). A study of nursing students in the Midwest indicated negative attitudes toward homosexuality. According to the study, 52% reported that lesbianism was unnatural, 34% thought it was disgusting, and 23% believed it to be immoral (Randall, 1989). More recently, a study conducted by the Gay and Lesbian Medical Association indicated that 67% of the 711 lesbian, gay, and bisexual physicians and medical students who responded to a survey knew of patients who had received substandard care because of their sexual orientation and 88% had heard their colleagues disparage their gay and lesbian patients. Of these physicians, 17% reported being refused medical privileges, fired, or denied employment, educational opportunities, or promotions because of their sexual orientation; 56% of the physicians reported experiencing some form of economic or social discrimination (Schatz & O'Hanlan, 1994).

Apparently, homophobia and heterosexism pervade medical and nursing education as well. Many lesbian and bisexual medical students have reported being denied admission to medical school or residencies and being ostracized or harassed by fellow students and supervisors (Schatz & O'Hanlan, 1994). According to a respondent in the Schatz and O'Hanlan study, one surgery resident was so rejected by his fellow students that he killed himself before he finished training.

Most health-related training does not adequately incorporate lesbian and bisexual issues into the curricula. Most medical textbooks, if there is mention of homosexuality at all, say nothing about lesbians and bisexual women while focusing on gay men and AIDS (Harrison, 1996). A study of medical schools in 1992 indicated that the average time allotted to this population during the entire medical training was three and a half hours (Wallick, Cambre, & Townsend, 1992). It has been found that a one or two hour lecture is the only formal training on the treatment of lesbians and bisexual women that health professionals received.

There are still many health care providers who are negative toward or do not understand homosexuals (Stevens, 1992). This is not surprising given the recent history of negativism in these fields. Herman (1995), Silverstein (1996), and Krajeski (1996) traced important history relevant to psychology and medicine and found that prior to the late 19th century, homosexuality was seen primarily as a moral weakness; homosexuals and homosexual behavior were condemned as a crime, vice, or sin. In the late 19th century, psychiatrists began to present homosexuals in case studies, labeling homosexuality a disease, proposing that it could be prevented or cured (although it was still also considered a crime or a sin outside of the medical environment).

From the late 19th century through the early 20th century, homosexuals (sexual inverts) were viewed as individuals whose psychological make-up and physical body were incongruent (what we now call transsexuals or people with gender dysphoria). However, the examination of feminine lesbians and masculine gay men poked holes in this theory.

In the early 20th century Freud had a limited impact on the way homosexuality was viewed. He hypothesized that homosexuality was not an illness, but rather a case of arrested development. All people were born with bisexual tendencies; the most healthy, however, developed into heterosexuals. But homosexuals, in his view, should not be viewed as sick or as criminal. In fact, he went so far as to advocate the removal of homosexuality from the criminal laws of Germany and Austria. Freud spoke primarily of gay men, but his work was generalized to include lesbians. His attitudes about homosexuality were not adopted by most psychoanalysts.

World War II had a tremendous impact on the ways in which homosexuals were viewed. Although, up until this time, there was no intense screening for homosexuality during recruitment, shortly into World War II, recruits were screened for homosexuality. However, women who strayed from gender norms generally were not screened out due to a need for women in the services. Prior to World War II, when homosexuals were discovered once in service, they were given long prison sentences. After World War II, they were sent for psychiatric treatment and/or to mental institutions.

During and immediately following World War II, there were psychological professionals who discovered how "normal" their homosexual patients were and became advocates for viewing homosexuality as an alternative sexuality rather than a mental disorder.

Kinsey's studies of the sexual behavior of 5300 men and 5940 women published in 1948 and 1953 indicated that there were much higher rates of homoerotic behavior than previously thought. He reported that 28% of women had erotic responses to other women by the age of 45 and 19% had some type of lesbian contact by the age of 40. Kinsey hypothesized that everyone had the capacity for homosexual behavior and that 10% of the population was homosexual. This number is still cited.

With the 1950s came a backlash against homosexuality. According to McCarthy, godless communism and perverted sexuality were the same types of evil and had to be eradicated. He and his staff listened to psychiatrists who told them that homosexuality indicated weak moral fiber and that homosexuals should not be in public positions. President Truman signed an executive order banning homosexuals from federal government positions and some public offices. The government backlash lasted until 1975, when the U.S. Civil Service Commission ruled that homosexuality could no longer disqualify men and women from working for the federal government.

In the early to mid 1950s Dr. Evelyn Hook obtained a National Institute of Mental Health grant to conduct a study comparing the psychological makeup of heterosexual and homosexual men. She found that experts could not differentiate the two based on personality traits and psychological tests. She presented her findings to the American Psychological Association's annual meeting in 1956. Her work helped to change the direction of research from searching for a cure, to looking for ways to deal with societal oppression.

In 1952, homosexuality was still listed in the Diagnostic and Statistical Manual (DSM) as a sociopathic personality disturbance, along with fetishism, pedophilia, and tranvestism. Treatments included psychoanalysis, aversive therapies, surgery, drugs, shock treatments, and even the insertion of electrodes into the brains of gay men. Treatments have been documented primarily for gay men. When treating lesbians, the focus was on teaching them to become more feminine as well as changing their sexual orientations.

In 1968 homosexuality was still listed separately in the DSM II as a sexual deviation under the category of personality disorders and other nonpsychotic mental disorders.

In the 1960s, activists started directly opposing psychological treatments for homosexuality. From 1969 to 1973 activists (community and psychological professionals) fought to have homosexuality removed from the diagnostic manual and viewed as a sexual variation rather than a mental disorder.

In 1973, after an intense debate among members of the American Psychiatric Association, homosexuality was changed from being listed in the DSM III as a sexual deviation for everyone who is homosexual, to "sexual orientation disturbance" only for those who were bothered by, in conflict with, or who wished to change their sexual orientation. Immediately following this decision by the Board of Trustees of the American Psychiatric Association, opponents of the change used a referendum process to attempt to overturn the action of the board. The decision was upheld by a 58% majority. It is important to note that, although officially homosexuality was no longer viewed as a mental illness, 42% of the membership of the American Psychiatric Association still viewed it as a mental disorder.

In the 1970s, gay counseling centers were formed in progressive cities around the United States, providing affordable support and counseling for lesbians and gay men who did not want to change their sexual orientation. These counseling centers not only provided treatment for gay and lesbian patients, but also provided a place for counselors to discuss their work with gay and lesbian clients.

Concurrently, literature on lesbian and gay health developed in both medical and psychological journals. The literature dealt with many issues, including the effect of homophobic external stressors (i.e., families, discrimination, parenting, civil rights), the effects of internalized homophobia, sexual problems, techniques for working with the lesbian or gay patient, barriers to care, sexual health, and the health of the children of lesbians, gays, and bisexuals.

In 1987, homosexuality was changed in the DSM III-R from its own category to one example of "sexual disorders not otherwise specified," in response to psychologists and psychiatrists pointing out to the board that the work on homosexual identity indicated that most homosexuals go through periods when they are disturbed by their homosexuality as a part of healthy development. However, at the same time, "gender identity disorder," a category that has been misused to treat young people who are or who will eventually identify as homosexual, was added.

Currently, there are both treatments which attempt to cure homosexuality and therapy for lesbian and gay people who are not interested in changing, but rather accepting their sexual orientation.

With increasing frequency, there are lesbian, gay, bisexual, and transgender caucuses or subcommittees in most medical and psychological organizations. However, homosexuality and bisexuality still remain illnesses in the international code book of disorders (ICD-9).

Many currently practicing psychological and medical professionals were trained during a period when homosexuality was considered to be a mental illness and illegal. Like the rest of society, they were often taught from childhood that homosexuality was immoral or disgusting. Although these issues are finally being addressed by professional organizations at conferences, through publications, and through the work of health activists, change is slow. And, because most medical schools incorporate little training about the concerns of lesbians and bisexual women, it is not surprising that many health providers are uncomfortable working with patients whom they know to be homosexual or bisexual, and that they are unaware of the heterosexual assumptions they make in their daily clinical work.

INTERNALIZED HOMOPHOBIA AND HETEROSEXISM: RISKS AND IMPLICATIONS

When a woman internalizes the homophobia that is all around her in society, it produces especially insidious results. Lesbians and bisexual women who view themselves as morally evil and inferior or who see their relationships with women as morally wrong may have feelings that are manifested by overt, self-destructive behaviors such as substance abuse, eating disorders, or even suicide, or by more covert manifestations such as lowered self-esteem that make them more likely to accept disparaging remarks or behavior toward them and less likely to feel that they can, or deserve, to succeed (Gonsiorek, 1993).

Most lesbians and bisexual women have certain levels of internalized homophobia, much of which is unrecognized. For example, students in a class on lesbian, gay, bisexual, and transgender health and culture, most of whom are gay, lesbian, or bisexual, read several anecdotes about people who experience gay-related violence. One of the anecdotes is about a heterosexual couple who was physically assaulted because they were mistaken by a group of teenage boys to be a gay couple. The physical abuse stopped only when the woman opened her shirt to prove that she was female. The students usually react by being upset and condemn the teenagers' behavior even more strongly than they did in their responses to other stories of gays and lesbians who are victims of more aggressive violence. Embedded in their attitudes is the idea that somehow the heterosexual couple did not "deserve it," which on some level implies that gays and lesbians do. It can be concluded that even among gay and lesbian students, who are in a supportive environment and interested enough to learn about the health of their community, there is the belief that they are guilty of doing something that is wrong. Similarly, even though research on the children of lesbians and bisexual women indicates that they are as well-adjusted as children raised by heterosexual mothers, many lesbians and bisexual women assume that they should not have children because it would be unfair to the children.

Positives among the Negatives

Although homophobia and heterosexism are clearly negative and damaging, they can spur action that can have positive results. To protect itself, the lesbian and bisexual women's community must create social support, activities, friends, family, advocacy, and even employment and legal aid. Many women participate actively in the community and have found a sense of belonging and comfort not found elsewhere in their lives. Events centering around gay pride create a tremendous amount of validation for the lesbian or bisexual woman.

Overcoming homophobia can be used as a step in the right direction in overcoming other types of discrimination. Although most anti-homophobia trainings deal specifically with issues relevant to sexual

minorities, they should be grounded in learning to overcome oppression.

⫷ IMPLICATIONS FOR
HEALTH PROFESSIONALS

✦ Once homophobia and heterosexism are acknowledged, it is
then possible to take the next steps to facilitate relationships with
lesbian and bisexual patients.

✦ The medical interview or medical history form is the first chance
to make the lesbian or bisexual woman feel comfortable and to
begin to facilitate communication. All materials that are provided to the new patient, client, or job applicant should be
gender neutral and appropriate for women of all sexual orientations and gender identities.

✦ When providing care for the lesbian or bisexual patient, if she
expresses concerns about discrimination (e.g., job discrimination
or housing discrimination), it may be appropriate to refer her to
lesbian organizations or for counseling to cope with the health
effects of the discrimination. Keeping updated about these resources is useful.

✦ All educational materials should be appropriate for women of
all cultures, including but not limited to lesbians and bisexual
women.

✦ Sexual orientation should be included in all anti-discrimination
policies. Slurs and insults about homosexuals should be treated
the same as any other racial, ethnic, or disability slur.

✦ Lesbian and bisexual patients, clients, and staff should be as-
sured of confidentiality. If you are going to ask them directly
about their sexual orientation, it is critical that they know how
much of the information will be protected.

✦ Staff who are uncomfortable dealing with lesbians or bisexual
women should not continue to be involved in their treatment
until they become more comfortable.

✦ If you are unsure about how to deal with issues related to sexual orientation that arise, ask for help from appropriate professionals or organizations (see Appendix B for a partial listing).

✦ When a victim of a homophobic hate crime arrives at an emergency room or comes to her physician with injuries, clearly, her physical safety is the first concern. However, it is also critical to create a safe emotional environment for her. Heightened sensitivity to issues of sexual orientation and the woman's feelings prevents "revictimization" and avoids increasing feelings of vulnerability or shame.

✦ The health provider, if she or he is the first person to talk to the victim of a hate crime, should encourage her to report the violence to the proper authorities. There are national organizations (and some local ones) that a woman can contact to talk about the decision to report the violence and to gain support during this process (see Appendix B).

✦ One common response to hate violence is for the victim to feel responsible for the attack and her injuries. The health care provider, who may be her first contact after the violence, can play a significant role by not feeding this guilt and by assuring her that she was a victim and that she cannot be blamed.

4

Identity

———— ℮ ————

Sarah

Sarah, at the age of 5, feels "different" from her peers. She is "less feminine" than her younger sister and refuses to wear dresses or play with dolls.

As she begins high school, although she dates boys, she does not understand what all the fuss is about. Rather, she misses the closeness that she used to have with her female friends. Throughout high school she feels that she does not belong and becomes isolated. She has a limited social life with few friends.

In her first year of college, Sarah establishes a very close relationship with her roommate and recognizes sexual feelings toward her. She thinks about her roommate even when she is sexually active with boys. She questions whether she may be a lesbian, but quickly denies it. She does, however, become close with Melissa, an "out" lesbian, and meets some of Melissa's friends.

In her second year at college, Sarah begins to have recognizable sexual feelings for one of Melissa's friends. She starts to read about lesbianism, and begins to believe that she is a lesbian. She spends more and more time with Melissa and the other members of the campus's gay and lesbian organization.

Sarah becomes involved with Melissa's friends and has her first sexual and romantic relationship with a woman. She now tolerates her feelings for women although she hopes that someday she will change. Nevertheless, she becomes more involved in the gay and lesbian group and joins a "coming out" group for lesbians coming to terms with their identity. As she becomes more involved in the lesbian community, she feels better about her sexuality. She identifies herself as a lesbian to her family and close friends.

As Sarah confronts negative reactions from her heterosexual friends and family, she becomes angry at heterosexuals in general and becomes more immersed in the lesbian community. She cuts her hair short, and often wears pink or black inverted triangles, a black leather jacket and slogans expressing her identity and her beliefs ("Hate is not a Family Value," "Lesbian and Proud"). She joins the Lesbian Avengers, a political activist group. She distances herself from her family and heterosexual friends. Almost all the people in her life know that she identifies as a lesbian.

After several years, Sarah realizes that not all heterosexuals are bad. Her change in attitude is, in part, a reaction to her family's change in attitude about her sexual orientation. She restrengthens her relationships with her family and her heterosexual colleagues. She becomes selective about the disclosure of her sexual orientation, carefully weighing risks and benefits. In addition to continuing her membership with the campus gay and lesbian group, she joins a group for female graduate students, and a group for Jewish students.

———————— ℮ ————————

*S*arah's experiences are not uncommon and are well described by the homosexual identity model proposed by Cass (1979) and substantiated with research by Cass in 1984. In stage one, *identity confusion,* Sarah knows that she is different, but she is yet to discover that this difference is due to her sexual orientation. Her confusion may lead her to destructive acting out or depression.

In stage two, *identity comparison*, she may act on her internal conflict—thinking that perhaps she may be a lesbian, and yet, knowing the negative ramifications of identifying as such—by using alcohol or drugs or even by considering or attempting suicide. She may also be at risk for sexually transmitted diseases as she tries to assert her heterosexuality. In either of these stages, she will probably hold back from talking with her provider about her sexuality.

In stages three and four, *identity tolerance* and *identity acceptance*, she risks rejection and a lack of support from her family and heterosexual friends. In addition, given that she has just taken on an identity that is often hated by the mainstream, she may take her mixed feelings out on herself in self-destructive ways. During these stages, she may be willing to talk to her providers about her thoughts and conflicts allowing him or her to recommend supports in the lesbian and bisexual women's community.

During stage five, *pride*, when she is involved as a lesbian activist in the community, she risks further rejection and perhaps is more likely to be perceived as lesbian and face anti-gay violence. As she becomes involved in the lesbian community, she may conform to cultural norms, which may include more substance and drug abuse. If her provider does not recognize her lesbianism, and in general, does not acknowledge lesbians through the use of gender neutral forms or materials, the provider can impede an open and honest relationship and discourage her from returning for care.

Finally, during stage six, *identity synthesis*, her health risks due to her sexual orientation decrease, although some health risks still exist. She is no longer confused, nor has she rejected all supports in the heterosexual community. She also chooses to pass as heterosexual when it is physically and emotionally unsafe for her to be out. During this stage, she will probably disclose her sexual orientation when it is relevant. It is important for her provider to be respectful and have resources available for support and referral if necessary.

⫷ IDENTITY MODELS

Researchers and theorists have proposed other models to explain the processes by which lesbians and bisexual women understand their sexuality, come to identify as lesbian or bisexual, and disclose this information to others. All of these homosexual identity models are grounded in the assumption that this process occurs against a backdrop of stigma that affects every aspect of the developmental process.

Although the early models focused on the dichotomy between homosexual and heterosexual, recent theorists have proposed similar theories explaining the development of a bisexual identity (Weinberg, Williams, & Pryor, 1994). Some of the early theorists have also indicated that their models may be appropriate for bisexuals as well as lesbians. It is important to keep in mind that all of these models have been hypothesized and tested only for western culture in the late 20th century and therefore may not be applicable across cultures and time (Cass, 1996).

The earlier psychologically based stage models are linear; the movement to advanced stages is contingent upon coming to terms with earlier stages (Cass, 1979). With each stage comes (Cass, 1996)

1. Increasing use of the concept of homosexual, lesbian, or gay to account for and understand the self

2. Use of terms "lesbian" or "gay" as an explanation of self within an increasingly wider number of interpersonal interchanges

3. Development of increasingly positive feelings about being a lesbian or a gay man

4. Increasing belief that one belongs to the lesbian or gay social group and strengthening social ties with other lesbians or gay men

5. Gradual acceptance of positive values about homosexuals as a social group

6. Increasing independence from heterosexual values

7. A gradual shift in use of concept of homosexual, lesbian, or gay from a means of labeling self to a description of an inner belief in self (p. 232)

In contrast, some of the more contemporary stage models are more flexible in structure than Cass's original model (Troiden, 1989). In these models, the individual moves back and forth between the stages and/or passes some stages altogether. Troiden (1989) presents a helpful metaphor:

The process of homosexual identity formation is likened to a horizontal spiral, like a spring lying on its side. Progress through the stages occurs in back-and-forth, up-and-down ways; the characteristics of stages overlap and recur in somewhat different ways for different people. In many cases, stages are encountered in consecutive order, but in some instances, they are merged, glossed over, bypassed, or realized simultaneously. (p. 48)

Alternatively, theories based on social constructionism propose that the identity of the individual is formed and changes based on their interactions with their environment (Ponse, 1977). Social identity theory can also help explain the process by which individuals and social groups are characterized and compared, and the ways in which individuals and groups deal with or attempt to change their homosexual status and their status in other minority groups (Cox & Gallois, 1996).

✑ ADDITIONAL STAGE MODELS

———————ℰ———————

Beth (Coleman, 1981)

Stage 1 (Pre-coming Out)

Beth, from an early age, has had close physical relationships with women. However, she has not heard of the word "lesbian" and does not think much about her feelings for women. Even when she reaches adulthood, she does not think about her physical longings to be with women, rather, she thinks about them as close friendships.

Stage 2 (Coming Out)

When Beth, 32, hears a lesbian speak about homosexuality on a talk show, she identifies with the speaker and begins to wonder if she is lesbian. She finds books on the subject, most of which emphasize the negative. One of her favorite female characters on television comes out as a lesbian and has a relationship with another woman. Beth thinks more about these events and believes even more strongly that she may be homosexual.

Stage 3 (Exploration)

Over the next few years, Beth begins to explore her sexuality and has a sexual relationship with a female friend. At the same time, however, she has sex with a male friend. She discloses her lesbianism to her family, and is told that eventually she will meet the "right man."

Stage 4 (First Relationship)

After several short, personally unsatisfying sexual relationships with women, Beth meets a woman with whom she has a lot in common and starts a more permanent relationship. They see each other for two years, during which they become extremely close and spend most of their time together. Over time, however, problems surface; they start having trouble communicating and spend very little time with other friends and family. Beth allows her work to decline. When the relationship breaks up, she is devastated and has to rebuild her prior relationships with family and friends.

Stage 5 (Integration)

After six months of therapy, Beth meets another woman with whom she becomes involved. This time, she does not exclude her other friendships. She is promoted at her job. Her lesbianism is a positive part of her identity and while her partner is important, she continues to pay attention to other parts of her life.

Beth's experiences fit a model proposed by Eli Coleman in 1981. Unlike some theorists, Coleman identifies potential health risks for each stage. During the pre-coming out stage, Beth feels isolated and may have low-self esteem. Because she does not know where her feelings are coming from, she may communicate the conflicts through behavior problems, psychosomatic illnesses, or suicide attempts.

During the coming out stage, Beth deals with rejection from family and friends and may be at risk for substance abuse, depression, or other unhealthy practices. She may be hesitant to develop an honest relationship with her provider for fear of further rejection, especially if she believes her provider to be judgmental. Exploration is often described as similar to adolescence, regardless of her age, and during this period Beth may be at risk for sexually transmitted diseases.

During her first relationship, Beth closes herself off and limits her support system. She may avoid her health care provider entirely for fear of him or her learning about her relationship.

Finally, during integration, although her confusion is minimized, she is at risk for reacting to the high stress level of being lesbian in a heterosexual environment and for discrimination from others. During this time, she is likely to weigh the consequences of disclosing her sexuality to her provider. If the provider asks appropriate questions and shows sensitivity, Beth is more likely to be open about her life and disclose relevant health information.

Stage models are helpful in describing "general patterns encountered" (Troiden, 1993) by committed homosexuals. They are "frameworks for ordering observations logically. . . . At best, ideal models capture general patterns; variations are expected and explained . . ." (p. 194)

Identity models may help health professionals think about where the patient is in her development and treat her appropriately. However, it is critical to keep in mind that these models provide only general frameworks and that most lesbian and bisexual women's experiences cannot be perfectly explained with linear models. Making assumptions from these generalities can impede the provider-patient relationship.

While Coleman's model (1981) is loosely based on psychological development and experiences from dealing with gays and lesbians, Cass's model (Cass, 1979) is grounded in the Interpersonal Congruency Theory; where stability and change in human behavior depend on congruency between the self and the environment. To Cass, homosexual identity formation is the process by which self-perception, behavior, thoughts and feelings, and one's perception of others' view of their sexuality become congruent.

At each stage, either the individual balances these areas, or foreclosure results and the development stops or recedes. Had Sarah not met "out lesbians" and had she continued to receive only negative responses from her family or friends, or if she was a member of another social group (i.e., a religious group or a racial/ethnic group) who she felt could not accept her sexuality, then she might not have been able to get beyond identity tolerance. She might have then chosen not to act on any future feelings for women and might or might not have been able to live her life with men rather than women. Rather than focusing on balancing the matrix, Coleman's model focuses on relationships.

Tanya (Weinberg, Williams, & Pryor, 1994)

Tanya, in her late 20s, is heterosexual when she becomes active in the feminist movement. During this time, she participates in events, consciousness raising groups, and protests, fighting for the rights of women and people of color. There are several women in her new group of friends who consider themselves to be lesbian. Tanya begins to question her relationship with her boyfriend and the way that women are treated by black men in general. She feels a lack of respect as a woman and questions her participation in a patriarchal system. However, she is still sexually attracted to her boyfriend.

Tanya breaks up with her boyfriend and develops a particularly close and eventually sexual relationship with a self-identified lesbian. Tanya begins to identify as lesbian, but hides this part of her life from her family and the black community. Although she enjoys her relationship with this woman, she still finds she is sexually attracted to men.

After a year, she breaks up with her female lover and begins a relationship with a man who is also active in the feminist movement. She still identifies herself as lesbian, in part because of pressure from her lesbian friends and her political convictions. She keeps her new relationship hidden from her lesbian friends, but is finally able to share her relationship with her family. She allows her family to believe that she is heterosexual.

After several years, Tanya and her boyfriend become engaged. Around this time, she reads an article in the mainstream press about bisexuality and begins to wonder if she is bisexual. She misses the closeness that she used to feel with women.

She and her fiancé disagree over the time she spends with her lesbian friends and they break up. Tanya spends a year without a partner of either sex. She starts reading what little she can find about bisexuality. When she tells them, both her heterosexual and lesbian friends reject her choice. Eventually she meets a bisexual woman and attends a conference on bisexuality. For the first time in her life, she feels comfortable and supported.

Tanya dates both men and women, depending more on the person than on the gender. She believes she could be happy in a long-term relationship with either a man or a woman. She feels she has tremendous support in and identification with the lesbian, gay, bisexual community.

Weinberg, Williams, and Pryor (1994) propose, in their book on bisexuality, a general stage model for bisexuality. First, they propose, bisexuals are *confused*, either because they have accepted a lesbian or gay identity and now are attracted to the opposite sex, or because they have always found themselves attracted to the opposite sex and are now attracted to both sexes.

Next, Weinberg, Williams, and Pryor propose, bisexuals begin to identify with the bisexual label. This can be precipitated by attending an event, meeting a bisexual person, admitting attractions to both sexes simultaneously or for some, hearing the term for the first time.

After *finding and applying the label*, bisexuals *fit into the label*. For some this is a quick process, whereas for others, it can take years. Having connections with other bisexuals can help with this process.

Finally, they propose that bisexuals remain in *continued uncertainty*. The pressure to categorize oneself into one end of the heterosexual/ homosexual dichotomy or the other is so strong that it is difficult to maintain the bisexual identity. Although this is certainly true for some women, other women, with support from the community, become comfortable with their bisexual identity. Most important, in Weinberg, Williams, and Pryor's model, the emphasis is on bisexuality as the goal of development rather than part of the process toward becoming homosexual.

Critiques of the Stage Models

Although there are many women whose experiences are similar to Sarah's or Beth's and for whom stage models help trace their development, these linear models do not trace the experiences of all lesbian and bisexual women. Stage models include several other critiques.

1. Most women have a continuous coming out process that fluctuates between stages for a large part of their lives. The stage

models do not explain women who identify as lesbian stronger in some circumstances than in others.

2. There are women who halt the developmental process without identifying as lesbian with or without continuing their sexual relationships with women. This foreclosure of the identification process does not necessarily lead to negative self-esteem.

3. The research supporting stage models has been conducted primarily with white, middle class, self-identified gay men and lesbians.

4. None of the models adequately accounts for and explains the interaction with other identifications such as race or ethnicity, religion, gender, class, and age.

5. In most of the studies, the data were collected and then the stages conceptualized. It is possible that the subjects may have been forced into stages.

6. Bisexuality has not been addressed well in most of the models or the theories.

7. The goal in most of the identity models is to have a well-integrated identity, with the lesbian or bisexual identity being one of many focuses. However, for some, the lesbian or bisexual identity remains a focus. It can be argued that activists, for example, have a well-integrated identity even though their lesbianism or bisexualism remains central to their identity.

Lee (Ponse, 1977)

Lee is the only child in a Chinese-American family. Whereas her mother immigrated so she could marry her father, her father immigrated as a young man. They live in a Chinese neighborhood in New York with one grandparent and two of her first cousin's families. When Lee reaches dating age, her family strongly encourages her to find a Chinese boyfriend.

Lee decides, against her family's wishes, to turn down an education at Columbia to attend an all-female university. While at college, she falls in love with a woman and has her first sexual encounter. However, she feels intense anxiety and guilt, cannot deal with the relationship, and leaves school. She feels guilty about shaming her family, goes home, and enrolls in a local city college without offering any explanation to her family or to her lover.

The next year, she starts at Columbia and dates the son of her parents' friend. She decides to wait to have a sexual relationship until after she is married. They become engaged.

On her wedding night, Lee panics when she does not enjoy the sexual relationship. She begins faking her sexual satisfaction. She often thinks about the nights with her only female lover, although these thoughts are coupled with guilt and anxiety. She knows that she is a lesbian but having a relationship with a woman is not possible for her.

Lee spends 25 years in this marriage and does not pursue a relationship with a woman until she is in her late 40s, after the unexpected death of her husband. She meets a woman who is also in her 40s and they fall in love. They spend time with several female couples and occasionally attend events in the gay and lesbian community. They live together until Lee dies in her late 70s.

-------- ℮ --------

Rather than stages, Ponse (1977) suggests a trajectory theory, grounded in social constructionism (simply, women identify in a particular way based on their interaction with the environment). She proposes that there are five elements; (1) a feeling of being different from heterosexual women due to desires for women, (2) an understanding that those feelings could be labeled as "lesbian," (3) assuming a lesbian identity, (4) seeking the company of lesbians, and (5) engaging in an emotional or sexual lesbian relationship. These trajectories vary based on the woman's interaction with her environment. Women may start with any of these trajectories and then move from one to another, or experience them simultaneously. Accepting the lesbian identity marks the final part of this process.

Ponse also acknowledged, unlike some of the other theorists during her time, that there were contradictions and complications to a stable lesbian identity. She identified four types of women; (1) lesbian identity and lesbian activity, (2) lesbian identity with bisexual, heterosexual, or celibate activity, (3) bisexual identity with lesbian activity, and (4) heterosexual identity with lesbian activity.

Lee, in part because of the pressure from her culture and her own values, lived more than two and a half decades with a lesbian identity and heterosexual activity. It took seeking the company of other lesbians and seeking a relationship with a female lover, along with an understanding that her feelings could be labeled as lesbian, before she could establish a solid lesbian identity.

It is important for health professionals to recognize the role that the sociocultural environment can have on the individual's identity formation. In some cultures, having a relationship with someone of the same gender shames the entire family and is seen as a direct assault on them. Choosing to have this relationship, putting the self over the well-being of the family, can result in the lesbian or bisexual woman's losing the support of her family and the rest of her community. For others, especially those living in rural or conservative areas, the thought of dealing with the loneliness of having to hide a relationship with a woman for safety reasons, and to protect job and housing security, is more than the lesbian or bisexual woman can cope with and they choose heterosexual relationships.

⊰ SOCIAL IDENTITY THEORY

Ana

Ana, a 23 year-old Filipino woman, was adopted by a white American couple when she was a baby. Until now, she has always identified with her parents' culture, celebrating American holidays and attending American schools. At the age of 23, she meets another adopted Filipino woman and becomes intrigued with her background. She spends more and more time with her friend and her friend's family, learning about her background.

She obtains a job at a non-profit health clinic serving Asian Americans and enrolls in graduate school to study the health of Asian immigrants.

While in graduate school, she meets a white woman and falls in love. She soon identifies as a lesbian. However, she finds that her new circle of lesbian, gay, and bisexual friends are primarily white. Similarly, her

Asian friends are all heterosexual. She fears coming out to them for fear of losing their support and friendship. At the same time, she fears insisting that her Filipino culture be celebrated or recognized for fear of losing the friendship and support of the lesbian and bisexual community. She feels that she is forced to choose whether to identify with the Filipino or the lesbian community, but that identifying with both at the same time will lead to loneliness.

A few months later, an anti-immigration proposition is passed in her state, making it difficult for her agency to provide services for Filipino immigrants. Her identification with this community becomes stronger and she and her partner fight over the time she spends with her Asian friends and her inability to be a part of that aspect of her life. They break up.

She meets another white woman and reconnects with the lesbian community. Her lesbian identification is strengthened.

Eventually, Ana finds a national group of Filipino lesbians who put her in contact with a small support group in her area. With the support of these women, she feels more comfortable identifying as a Filipino lesbian.

Cox and Gallois (1996) proposed that social identity theory can be helpful in understanding the way the individual identifies as a homosexual by understanding not only the individual processes, but the effects that society has on these processes and the ways in which the individual processes affect the broader social environment. Social identity theory also incorporates more than just the homosexual identity. Both her sexual orientation and her ethnicity are critical to Ana's identity process. Two processes, social categorization and social comparison, underlie social identity theory.

Categorization

Individuals categorize themselves and others into social groups (social identity: I am lesbian and therefore share behaviors or ideas that allow me to belong to their social group). They also categorize themselves with characteristics (personal identity: I am lesbian and therefore have lesbian behaviors). The self-concept consists of both the personal and the social identity. This theory explains the women who do not identify as lesbian although they are sexually active with women.

A woman can believe that her relationships with women are a part of lesbian behavior, but that they do not necessarily have the characteristics or behaviors that lesbians as a social group have, and therefore, do not identify as lesbian. There are many women who fit this category.

Social Comparison

Along with categorizing themselves and others, lesbians and bisexual women make individual and group comparisons. Positive comparisons lead to higher self-esteem. Dominant groups control the hierarchy of the social comparisons. In our society, heterosexuals and whites are the social groups that control the social comparisons resulting in the need for lesbians and bisexual women either to engage in a social mobility strategy or a social change strategy.

Social Mobility Strategy

There are four ways in which the out-group (homosexuals or bisexuals) can move into the in-group (heterosexuals) without any real social change. Many lesbians and bisexual women fit into the following categories:

1. Capitulation—these individuals try to avoid all homosexual activity. Self-hatred may result. Often, these women go to doctors to cure them of their homosexuality.

2. Passing—These women separate their lives into two worlds, the heterosexual and homosexual world. They usually do not come out. Keeping their worlds separate can be extremely stressful and they live in fear that they will be found out.

3. Covering—These women will come out if they are asked, but generally try to cover their homosexuality.

4. Blending—These individuals see homosexuality as irrelevant to their lives. They will avoid discussing their homosexuality, but if asked directly, will not deny this part of their lives.

Ana initially tried to pass as heterosexual among her Filipino friends and hide the importance of her ethnicity among her lesbian friends, separating her life so that some knew that she was homosexual, while others thought she was heterosexual. This resulted in her feeling isolated and alone. Each of the strategies for social mobility, where the focus is on hiding or blending, is stressful for the individual. The more the health professionals understand the strategies of their patients, the better they will be able to understand the risks to their health and well-being and be able to communicate with them more effectively.

For example, someone who is covering her homosexuality will be more likely to talk honestly about sexual behaviors with people of the same sex and be open about her partners, so that she can protect herself with appropriate legal documents, than will someone who is passing or who is capitulating. In this case, it is especially important for health professionals to reassure everyone with whom they come in contact that they are open-minded about people of all sexualities. Someone in the capitulation category may want to be cured of her feelings toward people of the same sex even though there is no evidence indicating that these treatments are successful. Assuring confidentiality is critical for women who are trying to hide their sexuality.

Alternatively, women can engage in social change strategies. These strategies include; social creativity, which alters the basis of comparison between negative and low social groups to a higher social group; and social competition, which leads to real change, includes social protests and lobbying, and enhances group identity.

Women who choose not to hide their sexual orientation, may engage in these strategies. This may enhance their sense of identity and pride, but at the same time, puts them at risk for discrimination based on their sexual orientation.

⊰ IMPLICATIONS FOR HEALTH PROFESSIONALS

✦ Stage models can be useful to the health professional for thinking about the health risks and ways to treat lesbians and bisexual women at various stages in their development. When in early stages, the lesbian or bisexual woman may be at higher risk for unhealthy behaviors, mental health symptoms, and suicide. In the pride stages, the lesbian or bisexual woman may be more identifiable as lesbian and therefore at higher risk for discrimination and hate violence.

✦ Stage models are limited in that they do not take into account the complexity and social context of sexuality. Social constructionist models may help the health professional think about other relevant aspects of lesbian or bisexual women's lives.

5

Disclosure

———— ☙ ————

Joan and Her Parents

Mother (*looking directly at her daughter's short hair and rainbow T-shirt*): *Why do you have to wear your sexuality on your sleeve? You don't hear your father and me announcing our sexuality.*

Joan: *Imagine, if at work you mentioned Dad's name, talked about me, or mentioned being married, that you could risk being verbally harassed, fired, or even physically harmed? And furthermore, imagine that everyone assumed you were in a relationship with a woman. Think about how many times you would have to lie or else you would not be able to share any information about yourself. How do you think that would make you feel?*

Father: *I suppose she would just stay to herself.*

Joan: *Not only would she end up feeling isolated, but she would probably think that there was something wrong with her, that she was doing something wrong. The people around her would probably figure out that she was lying about something and then she would lose their trust. Throw in a couple of nasty homophobic jokes and you can see how she might start thinking about how bad she is.*

I've decided that I need to be "out." My being out encourages others to be out. I've tried living a lie, and I've ended up miserable. Besides, I love Kristina. I want to be able to talk about her and include her in my life. You are asking me to deny the most important person in my life.

───── ℮ ─────

*M*ost lesbians and bisexual women cannot be definitively identified by their physical appearance or by biological tests. Rather, they choose the time to disclose their sexual identity and their relationships with women to others (Stevens & Hall, 1993). As Joan's conversation with her parents demonstrates, lesbians and bisexual women face a multitude of issues in disclosing their sexual orientation. While a closeted life may shield them from direct condemnation, it can lead to low self-esteem, high stress, and internalized homophobia (Deevey, 1993). It can also result in their living a life of constant fear or panic that they will be found out and prevent them from gaining social support from other lesbians and bisexual women.

✂ LIFE IN THE CLOSET

Disclosing sexual orientation is seen by most theorists and researchers to be an important part of the developmental process for lesbians and bisexual women (Coleman, 1981). The positive effects of disclosure include development of a positive lesbian identity, satisfaction with the lesbian lifestyle, psychological adjustment, enhanced self-esteem and acceptance, and authentic interpersonal relationships. Coming out may provide access to support from the lesbian and bisexual women's community, and may allow them to include their female partners in their lives.

On the other hand, living in secrecy may result in the devaluing of the self, low self-esteem, and increased levels of daily stress. It may also impede relationships with others and result in the individual living a life of constant fear or panic that she will be found out. Studies of women who are self-silencing or who believe that they do not have a voice, show that they are likely to be depressed, fearful, or have diminished self-esteem (Jack, 1991). Living in secrecy may be particularly difficult when lesbians and bisexuals get older because they may lose their partner and/or their lesbian and bisexual network. It may also be difficult in rural or conservative areas where there are few supports.

≈ DISCLOSURE TO FAMILIES OF ORIGIN

Unlike most minorities who have much in common with their families, homosexuals usually have a different identity from their parents. Coming out to families may be the most difficult process that a lesbian or bisexual woman ever has to face. This process can be particularly difficult for lesbians and bisexual women of color or women from conservative religious backgrounds (Chan, 1993; Espin, 1993).

The lesbian or bisexual woman goes through a complicated process of deciding whether to disclose her orientation to her parents. She may not want to disappoint her parents, and may fear rejection and a loss of love and approval. She may not want to cause family discord. However, she may choose to disclose because she wants her parents to share her life experiences or she may want to differentiate her life from that of her parents. She may also believe that her love for her parents necessitates honesty (Kleinberg, 1986). Many lesbians come out to their parents because of their anger towards their parents' negativity or because they know that if they do not come out, they will not have any relationship with their parents. In addition, they may feel uncomfortable with their secrets, and once unburdened, they feel better about themselves. It is understandable that most lesbians and bisexual women hope that their parents will eventually understand and accept them (Murphy, 1989; Schneider, 1989).

"Coming out models," similar to the models proposed for the lesbian and bisexual woman, have been proposed for the parents of gays, lesbians, and bisexuals. The following scenario illustrates one such model.

―――――ℰ―――――

Carol and Tom

From the time their daughter, Andrea, was a toddler, Carol and Tom sensed that there was something different about her. She was very precocious and preferred to do things by herself rather than with the assistance of her parents or teachers. As she reached adolescence, she did not seem as "boy crazy" as her older sisters and had particularly close relationships with her female friends. On the walls of her room she had pictures of women, several of whom were body builders or on motorcycles. On one occasion, Carol walked in on Andrea and her best friend while they were leaning on each other and watching a movie. It struck her as unusual, but she quickly put it out of her mind.

When she was 17, Andrea revealed to her family that she was a lesbian and that she had a girlfriend. Her parents reacted with shock and horror. This precipitated a major argument, during which Tom insisted that no child of his could be "queer" and that she had better rethink her new relationship if she wanted to be part of his household. They stopped speaking to each other and for several weeks the tension built.

Over the next few months, Tom and Carol calmed down, convinced that Andrea was "going through a phase" and that she would soon find a nice boy to date and live "a normal life." Andrea continued her relationship with her girlfriend and joined a gay and lesbian youth group. She spent most of her free time with her friends, participating in lesbian and gay events and reading books about lesbians. Against her family's wishes, she came out at school and was constantly teased by her classmates and even by her teachers. She did, however, obey her parents' order not to tell her relatives about her newly recognized sexuality.

Over the next two years, Tom and Carol's anger was replaced with feelings of concern and loss as they realized that their daughter might never change her sexual orientation. They were very worried about the abuse that she was enduring at school and tried to relieve the tension at home by talking to her about her new life.

Although they were upset at having a lesbian daughter and that Andrea would have a difficult life, they tried to empathize with her. They were also upset about teachers and other parents confronting them about their abnormal daughter. They still had not told their families.

Slowly, their anger at their daughter was replaced with anger at society for its treatment of lesbians and gays. They joined the local chapter of Parents and Friends of Lesbians and Gays (PFLAG), and although they still would have preferred that Andrea find a husband, they resolved to work on their relationship with her and support her any way they could. Both Tom and Carol became more sensitive to the concerns of lesbians.

The experiences of Carol and Tom are described in a theory proposed by Strommen (1989). In stage one, *subliminal awareness*, they sensed something was different, but didn't know what it was. In stage two, *impact*, they were confronted with their daughter's sexuality. In stage three, *adjustment*, they tried to minimize the long-term impact by believing it would go away. In stage four, *resolution*, they began to accept the permanency of their daughter's sexuality and mourned the loss of her heterosexuality. Finally, in stage five, *integration*, they began to integrate their identification as a parent of a lesbian daughter and were increasingly supportive of her lifestyle.

Once again, this process is usually not linear; the parent can skip stages or fluctuate between them. Each parent can also be at a different stage, which can cause family tension.

Families of lesbians and bisexual women deal with their children's sexuality in various ways. Many parents respond initially by severing ties with their children. This is especially difficult during adolescence and can result in homelessness for the teenager. Some parents expend their energy trying to change their child's orientation, even after the lesbian or bisexual woman becomes an adult.

During adolescence, some parents try to force the child into therapy with a mental health professional or with a religious counselor. They may encourage heterosexual relationships even after the lesbian or bisexual woman has settled into a long-term relationship with a woman. Or they may continue to deny their daughter's sexuality even when directly confronted with it. Often, communities of color ignore their family member's lesbianism to protect their relationship (Espin, 1993). It is particularly difficult for parents who are religious to deal with the dilemma that is presented by a lesbian or bisexual child.

The parent may respond negatively for several reasons. They may fear social stigma for themselves or their child. They may feel responsible for their daughter's sexuality, blaming themselves for having had poor parenting skills. They may fear for the safety and well-being of their child. And they may fear the loss of a positive relationship with their daughter.

Given the significant effect of the parent on the lesbian or bisexual's own development, especially when she is young, it is important for the health professional to understand the relationship between the parents and the children and determine whether it is causing serious stress, or whether she can expect support from her family. The health professional can recommend to the parent support groups such as PFLAG or books to help them understand their child's experiences.

In addition, the biggest risk in child custody cases with lesbian mothers, or in contesting wills, or neglecting the partner in the case of the death of a lesbian or bisexual woman, comes from the biological parents. For example, in the Sharon Bottoms case, Sharon's mother sued and won custody of Sharon's biological child because Sharon was a lesbian and therefore was an unfit parent. Similarly, in the Sharon Kawalski case, after an accident that left Sharon paralyzed, her biological parents were successful in temporarily forbidding her partner, Karen Thompson, from seeing Sharon and participating in her treatment.

✂ DISCLOSURE TO HEALTH PROVIDERS

Most lesbians and bisexuals can choose whether or not to disclose their sexual orientation to their provider. If they choose to remain closeted, they will be unable to discuss their health within the context of their entire life and may feel isolated from their health care provider (Stevens, 1992). In addition, there have been legal cases where the partners of lesbian or bisexual women were not allowed to participate in the medical care of their partners, in part because the providers did not know that they were lesbians (Kendall, 1995).

Health care providers not only provide medical care, but also counseling about healthy behaviors and referrals to support services. If the relationship between the provider and the patient is not honest, then this may affect the ability to provide accurate information, include the partner in the treatment, and understand the full range of relevant behaviors (Dardick & Grady, 1980).

This may be even more of a problem for bisexuals and transgendered women because bisexuality and transgenderism are understood even less than homosexuality (Hutchins & Ka'ahumanu, 1991; Stryker, 1994). It may also be more of a problem for women of color and poor women who experience a greater asymmetry in interactions with their health providers (Stevens, 1993). Gruskin (1995) found that the lesbian and bisexual women in her study who disclosed their sexual orientation to their providers were more comfortable and satisfied with their care and went for preventive and screening exams more often.

Lesbians and bisexuals vary as to the extent of their disclosure of their sexual orientation to their health care providers. Studies have indicated a wide range of disclosure rates from 34% to 84% (Bradford et al., 1994; Bybee, 1991; Cochran & Mays, 1988; Dardick & Grady, 1980; Stevens, 1992; Zeidenstein, 1990). These rates may be influenced by past experiences and by the gender and orientation of the provider; lesbians who had positive past experiences and had a female doctor and/or a lesbian doctor were more likely to disclose their orientation than those who did not (Zeidenstein, 1990).

In addition, lesbians may be more likely to come out than bisexuals (Cochran & Mays, 1988). Women who are more comfortable with their sexual orientation are also more likely to come out (Robertson, 1992). Disclosure to the provider may have a significant effect on the women's attitudes about their health care. Dardick and Grady (1980) found that women in their study who came out to their provider reported being more satisfied with their care and had greater ease of communication.

Hitchcock and Wilson (1992) theorized from their qualitative study investigating lesbians' self-disclosure, that the process by which lesbians disclose their sexual orientation to their health care provider is quite complex, consisting of two processes, anticipatory decision making (based on past experiences) and interactive decision making (in response to their current relationship with their provider). Their subjects' decisions to disclose their sexual orientation were influenced by their comfort with their sexual orientation, relationship status, attitudes and beliefs about health care, past experiences with health care, past homophobic experiences, environment of health care, and relevancy of sexual orientation to the medical care (Hitchcock & Wilson, 1992).

Stevens (1993) investigated the relationships between lesbian and bisexual women and their health care providers. Poor women and women of color were represented in her sample. She found that many of the women in her sample had had negative interactions with health care providers and that they had developed several strategies to protect themselves. This included rallying support from other lesbians, screening their providers for heterosexist or racist bias, seeking providers from their race, ethnic group and sexual orientation, watching carefully for prejudice or discrimination, controlling the information that they present to the provider, bringing a witness with them, and challenging mistreatment. These strategies indicate a lack of trust in health care providers and a need for self-protection when trying to obtain help.

❧ IMPLICATIONS FOR HEALTH PROFESSIONALS

✦ Disclosing one's sexual orientation is a difficult and continuous process. Keeping one's sexual orientation hidden, especially from people who are close to the lesbian or bisexual woman, can create enormous stress.

✦ Creating an atmosphere in which the patient can disclose her sexual orientation may be an important part of an open relationship between provider and patient, resulting in the best possible care.

6

Multiple Influences, Accessibility, and Isolation

———⊙———

Val

Val, a 26-year-old Latina woman, described to her therapist the conflicts she and her lover were experiencing about Christmas dinner. She wanted to celebrate the holiday with her lover of two years, but she knew that her lover was more open about being a lesbian than she was, and that this openness would be offensive to her highly traditional and religious family. Val believed that her family knew about her relationships with women and chose to ignore them. She believed that the only way to have a positive relationship with her family was to allow them to remain in denial.

However, this felt uncomfortable to Val's partner, who believed very strongly in the importance of coming out, and whose work centered on gay and lesbian concerns. It also went against Val's politics; she was aware of the research that showed that the strongest determinant of whether a person would have a positive attitude about homosexuality was knowing someone gay or lesbian. The more people who came out, the better it was for the gay, lesbian, bisexual movement.

Val felt torn between her allegiance to her partner and the lesbian community and her obligation to her family and the Latino community.

Her therapist helped her to work through her priorities and try to come up with a way to be around her family without compromising her partner or her political beliefs. They also discussed her options in trying to be a part of two communities at the same time. Val's therapist recommended that she talk with other Latina lesbians and provided her with references for a national organization and several anthologies.

Alena

Alena, a 34-year-old woman confined to a wheelchair, typically accessed a women's health clinic. However, she developed symptoms of an infection and was unable to obtain an appointment with her regular doctor, so she went to a different clinic that she knew to be wheelchair accessible. The doctor diagnosed a urinary infection without assessing her sexual activity. Alena was used to people assuming that because she was in a wheelchair she did not have sex, but she was too inhibited to provide this information to the doctor without having been asked.

When the symptoms did not subside, Alena went to her regular doctor who knew that she was sexually active with women only. This provider discovered that she had cervicitis, not a urinary tract infection, and that it had probably been sexually transmitted. Her doctor offered advice on how to have safe sex with her female partner.

Anita

Anita, an African American woman, was very active in her community church. She had started the homeless program and spent many hours matching young people with volunteers from the community who could help them with their schoolwork. However, when members of her church found out that she marched in a parade on gay and lesbian pride day, she was asked to step down from her position.

Le

Le, an 18-year-old Chinese woman in her senior year of high school, arrived at the emergency room with a broken nose, bad bruises, and two broken ribs. The attending physician found out that she was injured during a fight at school. When he asked her what the fight was about, she looked down and refused to answer. A few weeks later she returned, this time having been beaten by several boys in her class. Her physician asked her for her home telephone number so that he could contact her parents.

Le burst into tears and refused to give him the information. He referred her to the on-call psychologist.

The psychologist learned that Le's trouble at school had been precipitated by several boys in her class when they found out about a relationship she was having with an older woman. She had not told her parents about her relationship knowing that, although they knew her lover, if she were to confront them with her orientation, she would not only lose their support, but perhaps her home and might be forced to give up the community that she had lived in all her life. The psychologist was faced with the choice of whether or not to confront Le's parents with the nature of her relationship or respect Le's confidentiality, knowing that she would continue to be in danger at her school. She contacted the principal of Le's school, who was aware of Le's situation. They worked out a plan for her to finish her final few months of coursework outside the classroom so that she could graduate; Le would not be forced to come out to her parents.

The psychologist also recommended that the principal speak with a homophobia awareness specialist.

Gillian

Gillian was diagnosed with bipolar illness at the age of 29, about 6 years after she came out as a lesbian. She knew that, although her medication had stabilized her symptoms, high levels of stress sometimes precipitated either manic or depressive episodes and that she risked needing emergency treatment to help stabilize her symptoms. She also knew that her partner should be involved in her treatment and that her family should know about her partner so that in the event of psychiatric hospitalization, her partner would be included in her care. To protect herself, Gillian had to come out to her family about her lesbianism, come out to her partner about her bipolar illness, and come out to her providers about both.

✒ MULTIPLE INFLUENCES

Lesbians and bisexual women are as diverse as all women. The multiple influences in their lives greatly affect their experiences, including their health concerns and treatment. Although each individual is unique, it is helpful to understand that there are generalizations and trends when dealing with lesbians and bisexual women from varying communities. In considering the following, however, it is important to think about the ties that each individual has to her own community and the degree to which she considers herself a part of the community, to assess the relevance of community characteristics to their lives (Greene, 1994).

It is important to consider the multiple influences in the sections that follow.

Multiple Discrimination

Lesbians and bisexual women often confront sexism and heterosexism from both the mainstream and from other communities with which they identify (e.g., ethnic, racial, disabled). In addition, many lesbians and bisexual women confront discrimination from within the lesbian and bisexual women's community. This discrimination can be overt, such as requiring that they show multiple identification to enter a club as opposed to one form of identification typically required, or subtle, such as limiting outreach to white, able-bodied, middle class women and allowing these women to dominate all activities (Nakajima, Chan, & Lee, 1996). Although many lesbian and bisexual women's organizations are becoming aware of the importance of diversity, unlearning bias is an extremely difficult process and takes an extraordinary level of commitment.

Relationship of Individual to Group

Individualist cultures, such as mainstream American culture, emphasize the importance of the rights of the individual. Conversely, in others, such as some Asian cultures, the importance of the group may take precedence over those of the individual. Whereas many white lesbians and bisexuals see it as their right to disclose their sexual orientation and to have equal rights, in other cultures, if the disclosure of the sexual orientation negatively affects the family or the community, it is not seen by the family, the community, or the individual to be her privilege to disclose this information. This compounds the difficulties in identifying as lesbian or bisexual (Garnets & Kimmel, 1993).

Gender Roles

Communities vary in their expectations of the two (or more in the case of some Native American cultures) genders. Since gender roles are often associated with sexual orientation, understanding the variation in gender roles can facilitate an understanding of the lesbian or bisexual woman's experiences.

During adolescence, changes in the body often dictate exaggerated gender role differentiation. Boys and girls who formerly played together are now expected to take on new roles. Young women who are seen to be masculine are often called lesbians or epithets used for lesbians such as "lezzie" or "dyke." Although the young people who use this terminology are often not clear as to its real meaning, it is frequently their first introduction to homosexuality and can cause stress and confusion for the young woman who is attracted to other women. It also creates an atmosphere where homophobia is accepted.

Ethnic and racial communities vary in their treatment of gender roles. In some ethnic and racial groups, such as some Latino and Asian communities, strong gender roles make it particularly difficult to be lesbian or bisexual. In these cultures, it is often expected that women be submissive, willing to defer to men, and that they accept their primary role of wife and mother. Lesbians can be seen as threats to these expectations (Garnets & Kimmel, 1993).

On the other hand, in communities such as some Native American tribes, especially those which are less assimilated into American culture, the fluidity in gender roles may be one of the reasons that lesbians and bisexuals are accepted as part of the community. However, many tribes have taken on more mainstream ideas about gender roles and negative attitudes toward homosexuality, and therefore, reject gays and lesbians (Greene, 1994).

Family

The way the individual interacts with her family and the importance of family in the community are important considerations when working with lesbians and bisexuals. In cultures where the family is particularly significant, such as in Latino, African American, and many Asian groups, the lesbian or bisexual woman often feels forced to choose between her family and her lesbian and bisexual supports. She may also feel extreme pressure to remain closeted. The family, for many women of color, helps protect against the effects of discrimination and, therefore, losing the family is particularly traumatic (Greene, 1994).

In many African American and Asian families, there is the tendency to accept the lesbian or bisexual family member as long as she does not disclose this information about herself. Her behavior may not be taken as seriously as her identity. This form of denial allows the family to maintain their condemnation of same-sex orientations and their connection with the lesbian or bisexual family members.

This may cause problems for the woman who is trying to accept her lesbian or bisexual identity or is becoming involved with the lesbian and bisexual community. It can also create difficulties in relationships where one partner is "out" about her sexual orientation and the other woman is closeted (Greene, 1994).

For women with disabilities, who are often reliant on their families for emotional and physical support, being lesbian or bisexual has its own difficulties. If she is not out to her family and is relying on them for mobility, then it becomes much more difficult for her to gain support from the lesbian or bisexual women's community. She may also not want to lose the support from her partner given the discrimination that she likely faces from the able-bodied.

Elderly women confront unique issues when dealing with their biological families. Those elderly lesbians and bisexual women who came out early in their lives, came out prior to or in the early stages of the lesbian, gay, and bisexual rights movement. They, therefore, did not have the kind of organized support and visibility that lesbians and bisexual women now enjoy. They had more to risk and were more likely to have kept their sexual orientation hidden from their families. Given that the elderly often rely on adult children for care and assistance as they become less able to care for themselves, isolation from their family can create problems gaining the support that they need. And, like the disabled, they are often seen as asexual by their families and, therefore, find it particularly difficult to come out to their adult children.

Religiosity

Most organized religions condemn homosexuality. This creates intense conflict for lesbians and bisexual women whose families and communities are religious or who themselves have been involved in an organized religion. They often find themselves having to deny their homosexuality to reconcile their religious beliefs, or they feel guilt or shame because of their attachments to women, especially in their early relationships.

Religion poses a particular problem for some Asian, Latina, Jewish, and African American women where religion is at the core of their culture. Lesbians and bisexual women often have to choose between participation in the religious and cultural events and traditions as a closeted lesbian or bisexual woman, or give up their participation (Garnets & Kimmel, 1993; Jones & Hill, 1996).

On the other hand, some Native American tribes see people who break gender norms or have differing sexual orientations as able to see through both eyes (two-spirited) and spiritually powerful. In these tribes, the lesbian or bisexual woman may be treated with at least as much respect as their heterosexual counterparts (Tafoya, 1996).

Lesbians and bisexual women may also feel uncomfortable accessing services, such as homeless meals and housing or Alcoholic Anonymous meetings, that are available through religious organizations or held in places of worship. This should be taken into account and discussed when referring the patient to programs with any type of religious affiliation.

Sexuality

Cultures differ in their openness about sexuality, in the acceptable forms of sexuality within their communities, and in the consequences for veering from these permissible sexual activities. In many Latino, Asian, and Native American cultures, it is not permissible for women to talk about their sexuality. This makes it particularly difficult for the lesbian or bisexual woman to be comfortable talking with her provider about her sexuality. Coming out in these communities may be seen as breaking cultural rules about what should and should not be discussed.

In some cultures, such as Latino and Asian, it is acceptable for women to have physical relationships with each other, and this is not seen as lesbian. The problems arise not from their behavior, but when they identify as lesbian or bisexual. Similarly, it is often acceptable for young women to have physical relationships with each other as a part of their sexual exploration. For them also, it is the identification as lesbian and the continuation of a romantic relationship that causes the problems (Gonzalez & Espin, 1996).

Sexual stereotypes often affect the individual's experience as a lesbian or bisexual woman. For example, women of color are often stereotyped as being exotic, whereas women with disabilities and elderly women are often stereotyped as being asexual.

ACCESSIBILITY

Accessibility to the lesbian and bisexual women's community varies among different groups. Groups such as youth, elderly, disabled, women who do not speak English, and women living in rural areas, often find it difficult to access organizations, events, or even find books about other lesbians and bisexual women.

Young people cannot gain admission into events that take place in bars if they are under the drinking age. They also often have problems with transportation. Similarly, people with physical disabilities and the elderly may have difficulties with events that take place in buildings that are not wheelchair accessible and do not have elevators. Rural areas tend to have fewer events and organizations than do large cities, and those that do exist can be difficult to locate (see Appendix B for national organizations which can refer the patient to local organizations).

Along with physical limitations, women of color, the disabled, youth, elderly, poor, and transgendered women often feel that they are not welcome at events or organizations. And when they do go, they find themselves under-represented, and therefore unlikely to return. Although this is a focus of many organizations and sponsors of events, it remains a problem.

ISOLATION

Isolation can be minimized by referring these women to groups with which they are most likely to identify. If groups are not available locally, there are national organizations which have conferences and meetings, books that have been written, and a multitude of resources on the Internet.

⤜ IMPLICATIONS FOR HEALTH PROFESSIONALS

✦ In some cultures, it is particularly difficult to identify as lesbian or bisexual. Standards which make it especially difficult include strong gender roles with the female being submissive and having her primary role as that of wife and mother, strong family ties to large families, strong religious affiliations to religions which condemn homosexuality, and a lack of openness about sexuality.

✦ Acknowledging multiple identities facilitates understanding and communication with lesbian and bisexual patients. Materials (i.e., posters, pamphlets, and educational documents) should reflect as much diversity as possible.

✦ Accessibility is often limited for many members of the lesbian and bisexual community and should be taken into consideration when making referrals.

✦ Many lesbian and bisexual women feel isolated from the lesbian and bisexual women's community and other communities with which they identify. Referrals to organizations, events, reading lists, and Internet resources may provide some relief.

7

Sexual Health and Domestic Violence

---◌◦◌---

Lynn

Lynn went to her gynecologist for her annual exam. Her doctor started with the sexual history. "Are you sexually active?" "Yes." "What type of birth control do you use?" "I don't use birth control." "Are you trying to get pregnant?" "No." Her doctor proceeded to explain various birth control options and encouraged her to take a handful of condoms.

Daniella

Daniella was the only one of her college friends who was not sexually active with boys. Most of her friends went to a Planned Parenthood office near their school not only for information about birth control, STDs, and rape, but also Pap smears and breast exams.

Daniella, on the other hand, did not go to a gynecological provider until years later, when her female partner suggested that perhaps she should take care of herself by getting a Pap smear.

Carolyn

Carolyn called her nurse practitioner in a panic. She had blisters on her lips, which she thought might be herpes and she had had oral sex with

*her girlfriend the night before. Her girlfriend said that lesbians were not
at risk for sexually transmitted diseases. Carolyn needed to know for sure.*

Mimi

*Mimi was HIV positive from a blood transfusion after a car accident.
She and her partner Cassandra asked their provider about the chance of
Cassandra's contacting the virus when they had sex. Her provider located
some case reports in the literature. However, he found that it was not
adequate to provide the information they needed to help them protect
themselves. He recommended that they contact the Lesbian AIDS Project
at the Gay Men's Health Crisis to obtain information. He also gave them
a list of numbers that they could call to order safer-sex paraphernalia
including both a sex catalog and a pharmaceutical catalog.*

Sandy

*Sandy, who was involved in an s/m relationship, went to a gynecolo-
gist to assess what she thought might be a sexually transmitted disease.
Rather than dealing with her complaints, the doctor spent her appointment focusing on the bruises she had received during consensual sexual
play.*

————— ❦ —————

*L*esbian and bisexual women's sexuality is
complex. There is tremendous diversity in
the choice of sexual partners, what they do
together, what they mean to each other, and the impact on their health.
Since health professionals provide much of the information and
treatment that women receive about the health effects of their sexuality,

about sexually transmitted diseases (STDs), and about unwanted pregnancies, understanding the range of sexual activity of all women is especially critical. It is equally important for health care providers to be sensitive to the impact that their patients' sexuality has on other areas of their health, such as their stress level, their social supports, and perhaps the potential for unhealthy behavior.

One of the greatest barriers providers face in understanding the sexuality of lesbians and bisexual patients is their preconceived vision of their sexual practices.

There are no safe assumptions. It cannot be assumed that a woman who identifies as lesbian has sex with women only, nor can it be assumed that a woman who is heterosexual refrains from having sex with women. In fact, several research studies targeting lesbians and bisexual women indicate that although 95% of the women surveyed identify as lesbian, 78% to 80% have had sex with men during their lifetime and 21% to 30% have had sex with men in the past 5 years (O'Hanlan, 1995).

Providers often make assumptions rather than asking direct questions and rely on false understandings that interfere in their relationship with the patient and may result in inaccurate diagnoses and treatment. Lynn's doctor not only made her feel uncomfortable, but because he assumed she was having sex with men, he did not assess her risk for a sexually transmitted disease, nor did he provide her with education to reduce these risks.

Sexual contact, regardless of the partners or timing, takes place within the context of one's present life and past experiences. Not only are partners brought into the bed, but so are parents, religious leaders, friends, ex-partners, batterers, teachers, safe-sex educators, the law, ethnic communities, and society as a whole. Besides people, there are a wide variety of feelings of pleasure and love. Sex can bring with it anger, guilt, nostalgia, discomfort, fear, embarrassment, sadness, and pain. Sex is a tremendously complex combination of physical sensations, emotions, fantasies, and thoughts. For people who challenge sexual norms—women who have sex with women—sexuality can be as tumultuous as it is wonderful.

In American society, "ideal" sexuality consists of sexual intercourse between a legally married man and woman. However, as Kinsey and his colleagues first brought to the forefront in studies of American men and women in 1948 and 1952, these ideals do not represent all behavior.

They do, however, greatly influence sexuality, including how the lesbian or bisexual woman's sexual experiences make her feel about herself and her partners, how she thinks others will feel about her, which sexual activities are legally protected and which are criminal, how much she is able to protect herself against STDs and unwanted pregnancies, and how much fantasy is allowed to become reality. In most cases, the woman learns in early childhood that overt sexuality is wrong. She is taught not to touch herself "down there," to play "hard to get" with the boys, and certainly not to think about having sex with other girls. For the woman who is attracted to women, regardless of whether she acts on her attractions or identifies as lesbian or bisexual, sexuality may be, at least initially, laden with feelings of guilt, repulsion, anxiety, and self-hatred that exist with and sometimes overshadow excitement and pleasure. Even if the individual herself has not internalized negative ideas about same-sex sexuality, she knows that if she shares these feelings with the people in her life she risks rejection. This may result in unhealthy behaviors such as substance abuse, promiscuity with men, or unsafe sexual behavior.

⊰ SEXUAL ACTIVITIES

Lesbian and bisexual sexuality is diverse and can change depending on the individual's feelings, social networks, the sociocultural context of theirs and their partner's lives, with whom they are sexually active, and their moral and religious beliefs. Some lesbians and bisexual women experiment with a wide range of sexual activities with many partners, while others refrain from sexual contact or choose few activities with one partner.

⊰ RISKS

Until recently, it was generally believed lesbians were not at risk for most sexually transmitted diseases, including HIV/AIDS. This belief, held by both lesbians and their health care providers was due, in part, to the ways lesbians were defined in the epidemiological research.

The Center for Disease Control (CDC) defined lesbians as women who have had sex with other women and not men since 1973. As discussed earlier, most women who self-identify as lesbians do not fit this category because they have had sexual relationships with men at some point since 1973. Furthermore, the CDC and most other researchers use a "hierarchy of risk" when assigning routes of transmission. The highest risk activity reported by the individual is assumed to be the route of transmission. For example, if a lesbian had had a blood transfusion, sex with a man, or used intravenous drugs, then it was assumed that she contracted the virus through those routes rather than through female to female contact (Chu, Hammett, & Beuhler, 1992). Although these methodological limitations were eventually made public to the lesbian community and to health care professionals, the myth of lesbian invulnerability remains (Chng, Havens, & Fasick, 1990, cited in Denenberg, 1994).

There has been little biological or epidemiological research focusing on the risk of STDs during female to female sexual contact. The research that has explored the safe sex practices of lesbians and bisexual women indicates that lesbians continue to believe that they are at low risk for contracting HIV/AIDS, although their behavior indicates otherwise. In a study in Texas, 68% of lesbians surveyed thought that lesbians were at none to low risk for HIV and 10% of the lesbians in the study reported having had unprotected sex with IV drug users.

In a study of 1086 self-identified lesbians and bisexual women, 21% engaged in sexual risk behavior without protection (i.e., sex with a gay man or sex with an IV drug user) (Einhorn & Polgar, 1994).

Research that has been conducted to date, reinforced by case studies (Monzon & Capellan, 1987) and clinical documentation (Denenberg, 1994) indicates that lesbians and bisexual women are at risk for many STDs, not only because they may engage in sexual activity with men and use intravenous drugs, but also through female to female sexual activity. Although low in frequency, Herpes virus and all types of vaginitis have been found in women who have contact exclusively with women (O'Hanlan, 1995; White & Levinson, 1993). Chlamydia, syphilis, and gonorrhea are rare, yet have been reported in lesbians who have been sexual exclusively with women (O'Hanlan, 1995).

Given that HIV has been found in white blood cells of vaginal fluids, menstrual blood, and saliva, reinforced by several case studies, some authorities have suggested that it is "reasonable to suspect that the virus is present and transmittable during lesbian sexual activity at times of menses, vaginitis (when more white blood cells are present), or during traumatic sex practices"(O'Hanlan, 1995, p. 113).

The risks that lesbians and bisexual women face are compounded by a lack of preventive care. Women identifying as lesbian tend not to access reproductive health clinics or ob-gyn providers, and therefore often do not receive the screening that their heterosexual counterparts do (O'Hanlan, 1996).

In general, lesbians and bisexual women should protect themselves against sexually transmitted diseases during the initial stages of their relationships until it is clear that neither partner has any STDs and they can be trusted to be monogamous. Women who are not monogamous should be encouraged to practice safer sex. With HIV/AIDS, it is recommended that women practice safe sex with new partners for six months after becoming monogamous, and then both be tested for HIV before they practice sex without barriers. This allows for the latency period. A woman can test HIV negative for up to six months after she contracts the virus.

◃ THE BASICS

———— ᧒ ————

Sandra and Jennifer

Sandra's parents were somewhat accepting of her attraction to women. They welcomed both women into their home and allowed them to stay in the same room as they did with her younger brother and his girlfriend. However, they were extremely uncomfortable with any physical contact between the two women.

Sandra's parents called soon after their Christmas visit. Her mother was upset about what she called Sandra and Jennifer "throwing their sexuality in her face." She insisted that she liked Jennifer and was willing to accept their relationship, but that she did not want to think about what they did together in bed. Sandra asked what they were referring to specifically, and her mother described the time she "caught" her on the back porch sitting on the swing with Jennifer's arm around her. She also noticed that they were holding hands when they went for a walk. Sandra apologized and said that they would "behave" next time.

When Sandra discussed this conversation with Jennifer, Jennifer pointed out that Sandra's brother and his girlfriend were physically affectionate in front of her parents, as were her sister and her sister's husband. Jennifer and Sandra did not visit Sandra's parents during the next two years, choosing rather to spend their holidays with their friends.

Female couples, like most heterosexual couples, enjoy kissing, hugging, caressing, and cuddling with their partners. In fact, research has indicated that, for many female couples, these activities are a focus of their sexuality. Whereas it is generally acceptable for a man and a woman to hold hands or give each other a short kiss hello or good-bye in public, when two females engage in these activities, in most parts of the U.S., it is seen as offensive and may even place the couple in physical danger. Even people who support gay and lesbian rights may be uncomfortable seeing physical contact between women.

Manual Stimulation

Manual stimulation, also called touching or hand crafting, involves digital-clitoral, digital-vaginal, or digital-anal stimulation. This is common practice among lesbian and bisexual women. While some women enjoy direct stimulation of their clitoris, others find this sensation too intense and prefer to be touched in other ways.

Risks

When stimulated, women emit vaginal secretions. These secretions can contain bacteria, viruses, and white blood cells and can allow STDs to be transmitted between women. Transmission can occur when the person doing the stimulating has cuts or abrasions on her hands. However, warnings to use protection only when one has visible skin breaks are probably inadequate, because the viruses and bacteria that cause STDs are extremely minute.

Lani Ka'ahumanu, a sex educator in San Francisco, recommends rubbing one's hands with a lemon. If there is any stinging, then there are openings large enough to serve as portals of entry for bacteria and viruses. When a woman touches her partner and then herself (or vice versa) during manual stimulation, STDs can also be transmitted from partner to partner. In addition, manual stimulation of both the vagina and the anus can result in tears or scratches.

Protection

It is highly recommended that all women, unless they know for sure that they are not at risk for STDs (they have been tested over the latency period and both they and their partner are monogamous), use latex gloves or condoms stretched over the fingers during manual stimulation. To prevent infection, it is important for women to change gloves when moving between themselves and their partners and when they move from the anus to the vagina. Finger cots, gloves, or condoms can protect against abrasive nails and rough skin. Latex gloves and finger cots can be purchased at sex stores, through mail order catalogs (see listings in Appendix B), and at some pharmacies. Nonlatex gloves and condoms are also available for those who are allergic to latex.

Penetration

Many lesbians and bisexual women, like heterosexual women, engage in a range of vaginal and/or anal penetration. Some lesbians and bisexual women engage in penile-vaginal or penile-anal penetration with men. Others prefer penetration with fingers, hands, (known as fisting), or other objects. While some women choose to use household items, others opt to purchase sex toys called dildos for this purpose.

Sex toys come in all shapes, sizes, colors, and materials. The dildo can be hand-held or attached to the woman by a harness, leaving hands free for other activities. There are even two-sided dildos that can be inserted into both women simultaneously. Dildos can be used for anal penetration as well as vaginal penetration, but "butt plugs" made specially for anal penetration have a wider base to prevent the toy from traveling too far up the rectum. Strings of anal balls are sometimes used to penetrate the anus. Plastic and rubber dildos are easier to clean than those of leather or clay and therefore safer from infection-causing bacteria.

Risks

Like heterosexual women, lesbians and bisexual women are at risk for STDs and pregnancy when practicing penile penetration with men. As with manual stimulation, penetration can result in the transmission of STDs or tears and abrasions. STDs can also be transmitted through the use of sex toys that are not sanitized between partners.

Protection

Lesbians and bisexual women engaging in sex with men should be provided with information about pregnancy and STD prevention. Gloves can be used to protect against STDs and abrasions during manual penetration. Lubricants should be used whenever penetrating the anus and whenever the vaginal secretions have not sufficiently lubricated the vagina. Water-based lubricants should be used with latex gloves and condoms because oil-based lubricants can cause breakage. In addition, many women are allergic to nonoxynol-9, a spermicide, and it may therefore irritate the vaginal area.

Dildos, butt plugs, vibrators, and other toys should always be covered with a clean condom and washed well after use. They should be shared between partners only after changing the condom. Similarly, toys should not be moved from the anus to the vagina without changing the condom or washing and sterilizing noncovered toys.

Oral Sex

Oral sex includes using the tongue and lips to stimulate the partner's body. Oral-vaginal sex, also referred to as "going down on someone," is popular among many lesbians and bisexual women. Some women avoid oral sex during menstruation, whereas others engage in these practices throughout the menstrual cycle. Oral-anal sex or "rimming," whereby one partner licks or kisses the anus of the other partner, is practiced by some women, regardless of their sexual orientation.

Risks

The likelihood of transmission of sexual diseases through oral sex is unclear; however, there is evidence of HIV, Human Papilloma Virus

(HPV), and other bacteria and viruses in the menses and vaginal fluids. It is possible that oral sex between women is a potential transmitter of certain STDs and vaginitis, especially during menses when more white blood cells are present and when there is bleeding. There is evidence that lesbians and bisexual women can transmit herpes through oral sex (O'Hanlan, 1995). Anal-oral sex carries a risk factor for hepatitis and venereal warts, as well as other diseases (Califia & Sweeney, 1996). There has been no research to date exploring the bacteria and viruses in female ejaculation, another potential risk during oral sex.

Protection

Female couples can protect themselves during oral sex by using a barrier between the mouth and the vagina or anus. This barrier can be created with dental dams, cut condoms or gloves, or plastic wrap. Glide dams, a thinner, larger, better tasting type of barrier, are becoming more available at sex stores and through mail order catalogs.

Tribadism

Tribadism is a practice also known as humping or rubbing. It involves one woman rubbing her vulva against the body of her partner. Although it is popular among lesbians and bisexual women, tribadism is rarely mentioned.

Risks

Tribadism, in itself, is a low-risk activity.

Vagina-Vagina Contact

Like tribadism, vagina-vagina contact is rarely mentioned and the frequency of this behavior is unknown, given that it is almost never included as an option in surveys of sexual activity.

Risks

Vagina-vagina contact may be an important route of STD transmission, since the vagina is a mucous membrane.

Protection

A barrier should be used when either partner is at risk for STDs.

⤜ POWER PLAY (SADOMASOCHISM)

It is unclear whether sadomasochism (s/m) is more common in the lesbian and bisexual women's community or just more visible among lesbians and bisexual women than heterosexuals. Regardless, it encompasses a visible community with its own sexual risks and concerns. Pat Califia, one of the first s/m activists, provides a clear definition of s/m:

> . . . *an erotic ritual that involves acting out fantasies in which one partner is sexually dominant and the other is sexually submissive. The basic dynamic of sexual sadomasochism is an eroticized, consensual exchange of power—not violence or pain. . .*
> *(Califia & Sweeney, 1996, p. 118)*

Definitions of s/m vary widely. Some women emphasize power, whereas other women emphasize pain. No matter how it is defined, s/m has negative connotations both inside and outside the lesbian and bisexual community. It is also often the most visible form of sexuality in these communities and may pose risks to the individual. People who identify with the s/m or leather community often feel that they are forced to stay closeted about their sexual identity to protect their jobs, their relationships with family, coworkers, and friends, and to protect themselves from the law (inflicting harm on another person, even when consensual, is illegal), and therefore are not free to talk about their sexual behavior.

The s/m community has been at the forefront in promoting and practicing "safer sex." There are enforced codes of activity at parties and books that clearly explain how to protect oneself emotionally and physically, in addition to community meetings, forums, and workshops in many areas of the country to learn how to play safely. However, s/m behavior is practiced by many lesbian and bisexual women who do not communicate with or participate in s/m communities. In isolation, the practices described may be dangerous emotionally and physically.

S/m activists often recommend that health professionals, especially those who do not have experience with this community, when they meet patients who practice these activities, refer them to organizations or to references so that they can learn how to protect themselves.

Communication and "Safe Words"

When engaging in any s/m activities, it is especially important for all participants to discuss their limits and negotiate safer sex in advance and throughout the activity. All partners should understand that when it begins to feel unsafe for anyone, an established "safe word" should stop all action, especially in the beginning of a relationship as the two partners learn about each other's limits. This safe word should not be a word that is likely to be uttered during the sexual activity.

Bondage

Bondage can be part of sexuality for people who engage in other forms of s/m and those who do not. It ranges from physically or verbally holding one's partner in a certain position to restraining her in a full body sling.

Risks

It is critical that women ensure that in an emergency (e.g., fire, earthquake), that the bonds can be easily untied. No one should be left tied up and unsupervised. Also, it is important that the bonds not be too tight. Bondage can result in a loss of blood to limbs, rope burns or cuts, nerve damage, and suffocation. Joints can also be damaged.

Protection

The "toys" such as padded leather cuffs that are made specifically for bondage are usually physically safer than regular handcuffs or homemade equipment. However, there are knots that can be easily untied in case of emergency. People participating in the bondage should practice until they are efficient at tying and untying each other. Silk scarves and nylon rope should be avoided by the novice; silk is difficult to untie in case of emergency and nylon easily slips into tighter knots.

Cuffs which do not lock in place should also be avoided. Care should be taken with bonds around wrists and ankles so as not to damage the joints. Necks should not be bound in paraphernalia that does not lock or fasten securely into place, and care should be taken to make sure that, when gagged, the bound person can breathe easily through her nose. If it appears that a patient has been bound in a dangerous way, references to books or s/m organizations or a brief description of these guidelines can be helpful.

Pain

Some women enjoy painful sensations, including spanking, whipping, physical exertion, paddling, or cutting, during sexual activity. Health care providers might notice welts, scars, cuts, or bruises. These may indicate consensual s/m or they may be markings of domestic violence. Sensitive questioning and an examination of the physical marks as well as sensitivity to emotional responses should help the provider to differentiate. Neat, controlled markings on the safe areas— buttocks, shoulders, upper arms, breasts, or thighs—generally indicate safe practices, and if consensual, are often signs of an s/m relationship. On the other hand, marks on the face, spine, extremities, especially from a defensive posture or the stomach may be signs of battery. Asking direct questions will often yield truthful answers, especially if the woman believes the health professional to be nonjudgmental.

Risks

Striking the head, throat, neck, stomach, spine, kidneys, joints, lower calves, or shins can cause permanent damage. Any blood sports (e.g., tattooing, piercings, cutting) put the partners at risk for HIV/ AIDS, if either partner is HIV positive, or for other types of infections.

Protection

Lessons and practice in s/m techniques are encouraged by s/m activists. In addition, participation in the s/m community may help the individuals protect themselves from involvement with someone who is dangerous or careless. The members of the s/m community often warn each other when they have experienced a negative interaction, and they are aware of their safety at their sex parties.

✑ TAKING A SEXUAL HISTORY

The sexual history is an important part of the providers' assessment of their patients' health risks and experiences. However, most physicians are not trained to conduct interviews that will elicit information about same-sex sexuality or other nontraditional sexual activity.

It is important for providers, when conducting sexual interviews, to make the process as comfortable for their patients as possible. When the provider assumes heterosexuality, the taking of sexual history can lead to a web of lies and omissions. Providers, rather than assuming that sexual activity includes heterosexual vaginal intercourse, should ask specific, gender-neutral questions, demonstrating that they will accept anything, until the patient offers more specific information. They can facilitate this process by having information about a range of sexual identities and behaviors visible in their office through posters, informational sheets, and books.

Following are examples of gender neutral questions. Keep in mind that only the questions that are relevant should be asked so that the interview does not feel like an interrogation.

1. Are you sexually active?

2. Do you think you will be in the near future?

3. Do you think it will be with men, women, or both?

4. Do you have a need for birth control? What type do you use?

5. Is there any possibility that you are pregnant?

6. If with women, do you have oral sex? During your period? Have you been tested for HIV? Do you use a barrier? Do you use gloves or condoms? Are you monogamous? If not, how do you protect each other?

7. Have you had sex in the past with men, women, or both?

8. Do you ever practice oral/anal sex? Do you use a barrier?

9. Have you ever practiced s/m? Have you been given resources or information? Would you like some? .

10. Is there anything you would like to ask? Do you need any information or resources?

⚛ CONSIDERATIONS FOR HEALTH PROFESSIONALS

The more comfortable one is with sexual diversity, the easier it is to talk with patients about their sexual risks and concerns. If the materials in providers' offices (pamphlets, books, and posters) and intake forms represent sexual diversity, there may be a safe place created for patients to talk about their sexuality.

Women must be convinced that their lesbian identity does not protect them from STDs; their actual risks depend on their behavior. Lesbian and bisexual women are at risk unless they know that they and their partners are free from STDs (also allowing for the latent period), and neither is having sex without protection nor are they sharing needles. Lesbians and bisexual women should be encouraged to have regular gynecological exams, including Pap smears and breast exams.

Health care providers cannot assume anything about a woman's sexual behavior based on her identity and vice versa. Always ask direct questions for relevant information.

If there is any doubt about patients sexual practices, provide *all* patients with information about sex with women and with men. Many patients may not be open about their sexual activities.

⚛ SAFER SEX

Communication and negotiation between partners are key to safer sex. All women are at risk for STDs if they have not been tested since engaging in unprotected sex with either men or women who they are not absolutely certain are free from the STDs. All women are at risk for HIV/AIDS if they share needles with men or women who they are not sure are free from HIV.

No barriers are risk free—this includes condoms, dental dams, gloves, and plastic wrap. When one partner is at risk or there is any doubt, barriers should be used during oral-vaginal sex. Barriers should also be used during oral-anal sex. Condoms should always be used on sex toys and changed between partners or use between the anus and the vagina.

Gloves or condoms should be used on fingers and hands if one partner is at risk for STDs and to protect from the abrasion from nails and fingers.

Water-based lubricants should be used with latex. Oil-based lubricants can cause latex to break. It is better to use too much lubricant than too little.

Condoms should be used during sexual intercourse with men (anal or vaginal) when one partner is at risk for STDs or to prevent pregnancy. Barriers should be used during genital to genital contact if one partner is at risk.

If practicing s/m, women should be well-informed about risks and safe practices and find community support if possible. Women at risk should not share paraphernalia for blood sports.

⋖ DOMESTIC VIOLENCE

Andrea and Betty

Andrea was hiding a bloody nose when the police arrived. Her partner, Betty, told the police that they were having an argument, and they would keep it down. Andrea hid in the corner, knowing that if she said anything, Betty would let her have it later. As soon as the police left, Betty continued throwing her against the wall. Andrea made it to the mirror to look at the damage. She knew that, once again, her makeup would not hide her black eye. She also knew that her friends had noticed her bruises and she wondered why no one ever said anything to her or to Betty. The one time she had tried to tell a mutual friend, her friend denied that Betty was "battering" her, telling her that she could not take sides and that Andrea would need to learn how to protect herself. After another year of abuse, Andrea finally left Betty and made it to a shelter for battered women.

Cindy

Cindy, after running away from a female batterer, went to a shelter in the next town. However, one of the women in her social network told her partner where she was, and her partner was allowed to come to see her at the shelter, something that was strictly forbidden for male batterers. Cindy no longer felt safe and went back to her relationship.

Antonia

> *Antonia was in a verbally and emotionally abusive relationship with Charlene for three years before she started to think about leaving. Antonia was not out about her sexual orientation to her parents or her supervisor at work. Antonia, after a particularly degrading argument, decided to leave for a few days. During that time, Charlene called her parents, one of her coworkers, and her boss and told them about their relationship. Antonia's family was unable to cope with this news and stopped speaking to her for several months, at a time when she most needed their support. Fortunately, her supervisor continued to be supportive.*

As with hate crimes, it is difficult to estimate the scope of the problem of domestic violence in same sex relationships. Pamela Elliot reports that the current research indicates that between 22% and 46% of lesbians are being physically abused in same-sex relationships and 73% to 76% report at least one type of abuse. These numbers are comparable to those for heterosexual women (Elliot, 1996).

Even with this high prevalence, same sex domestic violence has, until recently, remained invisible. Perhaps the lesbian and bisexual women's community did not want negative aspects of their relationships to be revealed and it was not something that mainstream police and health care providers considered. Therefore, the treatment of both the victim and the perpetrator was as much of a problem as was the violence.

Domestic violence for both same sex and opposite sex couples includes physical abuse, sexual violence, property damage, threats, economic control, and psychological or emotional abuse. In addition to the behaviors similar to those in heterosexual battering relationships, in same-sex domestic violence, the perpetrator can use the individual's own internalized homophobia, as well as the homophobia of the other people in her life, to exercise control. For example, she might say negative things about homosexuality that she knows would deeply upset her partner and make her feel more ambiguous about her sexual identity. Or she could threaten to or actually tell her partner's boss or her partner's family about their relationship. As a result, the woman could lose her job or the support of her family, which is especially critical if she is thinking about leaving the abusive relationship (Elliot, 1996).

It is very difficult for the woman who is being physically, emotionally, or sexually abused by a woman to get help from the police, women's shelters, or health professionals. Most people have been taught that battering, when a man beats his wife or perhaps his children, is a heterosexual phenomenon. The lack of education about same-sex domestic violence is compounded by a desire not to think about women as being capable of violence. In fact, most theories on the causality of domestic violence are grounded in patriarchy and sexism.

Similarly, it may be difficult for the lesbian or bisexual woman being battered by her female partner to seek help in the lesbian, gay, bisexual, or transgender community for several reasons. First, these communities are small, especially in rural areas, and therefore, the victim may feel that other members of the community will be forced to choose sides or that she will lose her social supports. She may be aware that it is often hard for members of a small community to accept that there are those among them who are capable of committing violent acts on "family," especially if they know the person to be nonviolent in their other relationships. The survivor may have recognized clear signs from her friends to keep knowledge of the violence quiet as they ignore bruises and broken bones. Many times, the first person the victim approaches to talk about the violence is unable to deal with it; this makes the victim less likely to talk about it with anyone else. She may also know that if she tried to escape the batterer, she would have to leave her entire network of friends, as it would be inevitable that they would see each other at social events, organizations, etc.

Because it is difficult for many women and men to see women as perpetrators of violence, the survivor is often blamed for the violence. Whereas it is often unlikely for a police officer to assess domestic violence between a man and a woman, it is even more unlikely that they suspect domestic violence between two women and intervene to protect the victim. Similarly, in most areas of the country, if a woman being abused by a female lover attempts to receive help at a women's shelter, she may have a hard time having her experiences taken seriously. This creates another situation where she feels mistrustful and is likely to be victimized again. This has begun to change as same-sex battery has gained more visibility among health care providers and in the lesbian and bisexual women's community.

IMPLICATIONS FOR HEALTH PROFESSIONALS

- It is important for health care providers to create an environment where the survivor is not only comfortable talking about the abuse she is suffering, but also revealing the sex of the perpetrator.
- Equally important is understanding the potential ways a perpetrator can use both internal and external homophobia to control her partner.
- Think about the ramifications of the patient's reporting the violence prior to encouraging her to do so (e.g., being outed, potential loss of support from members of community, and potential negative reaction of the police).
- Health care providers need to make sure that the shelters that are being referred to women being abused by women are open to same-sex domestic violence, and that they will not treat the victim inappropriately.
- It is important to be sure that what the health care provider is seeing is clearly nonconsensual violence, rather than consensual s/m. Ask her how she got the marks, try to read body language and facial expressions. Some women have cellular damage without being in a battering relationship. If necessary, the provider should err on the side of protecting the patient from physical harm.
- It may be necessary to help the victim set up an appointment with someone who has experience working with survivors of domestic violence; once again, make sure that this person is open to domestic violence between women.

8

Legal Issues

*I*n most areas of the United States, lesbians and bisexual women, and those who are perceived to be breaking gender norms, can be fired, denied housing, lose their children, be skipped over for promotions, and be denied the right to marry their life partners without any legal recourse. Given that same-sex sexual activity was a crime in all states until 1962 and still is a crime in 22 states at the time of this writing, the prevalence of laws that negatively affect the health and well-being of lesbians and bisexual women is not surprising (Purcell & Hicks, 1996).

State and local laws that affect lesbians and bisexual women vary extensively. The extent to which these women may be affected differs also according to the available resources to hire legal assistance and the concurrent discrimination they confront.

The relationship between health professionals and their lesbian or bisexual patients may be affected either directly in health-related legislation, or indirectly as their lesbian and bisexual patients cope with the stress of dealing with the inequalities in the legal system. They may also find themselves in the middle of a dispute between their patient's family and her female partner when emergency medical decisions must be made.

Health professionals can help to prevent or to avoid these situations by advocating that same sex couples be prepared and by providing resources so women fill out the legal documentation to protect their relationship in the case of a medical emergency or death (see the legal section in Appendix A for information on resources for copies of forms). They can also serve as advocates for female couples in cases where they have not filled out the proper documentation and are facing a legal battle.

The five primary areas of law that affect lesbians and bisexual women are (1) criminal law, (2) civil rights law, (3) family law, (4) death and disability law, and (5) immigration law. Although discussed separately here, these areas overlap and directly affect each other.

CRIMINAL LAW

Michael

In July 1986, in perhaps the most devastating blow to the lesbian, gay, and bisexual community, the Supreme Court narrowly upheld the state of Georgia's right to enforce its sodomy law. During a drug search of Michael Hardwick's home, police officers found Michael engaged in sexual relations with another adult male and arrested him on sodomy charges. The Supreme Court ruled that Georgia had the right to restrain homosexual activity because of the "ancient roots" of the laws even though these laws seemingly infringed on Michael's right to engage in the sexual activities of his choosing in the privacy of his own home. Although legal scholars, including Justice Powell, who ruled with the majority, have questioned the validity of this ruling, it will probably be the precedence for some time in the future (Purcell & Hicks, 1996).

The legal system in the United States is based on the Common Law of England with sodomy laws that made homosexual behavior illegal. A little over half the states have opted to overturn these sodomy statutes either through legislation or through the courts, but lesbians and bisexual women are, by their assumed or actual sexual behavior, still criminals in the remaining 22 states.

The sodomy laws that govern the legality of behaviors vary from state to state; some states prohibit oral sex, some prohibit anal sex. Some states base their sodomy laws solely on behavior, whereas other states criminalize sexual activity between unmarried couples, including, but not limited to, same-sex couples. Regardless of the form they take, sodomy laws can be used to prohibit same-sex sexual behavior (Purcell & Hicks, 1996). Although it is rare for women to be arrested or cited based on the sodomy laws, they are often used as the basis for discrimination in other areas, such as custody cases or housing discrimination.

Besides their direct criminalizing effect, sodomy statutes and other subjective laws perpetuate discrimination and prejudice against lesbians and bisexual women, making it unsafe for them to disclose their sexual orientation, especially if they have custody of, or work with, children (Purcell & Hicks, 1996). As previously discussed, being forced to hide one's sexual orientation not only creates stress but also may keep women from providing health professionals with complete medical information and from accurately filling out medical forms, as well as the legal documents necessary to protect their wishes in the case of death or disability.

✄ CIVIL RIGHTS LAW

———ℰ———

Dr. Laklow

Dr. Laklow was up for tenure at a well-known university. She had been published widely in peer-reviewed journals in the areas of both lesbian health and other women's health issues. She was at the forefront of lesbian and bisexual women's activism, championing the rights of this group within her university and through her work at the state and federal levels. Her student reviews were excellent. Both she and her colleagues were shocked that she was not awarded tenure.

Marissa

Marissa decided, although she was very interested in the issues relevant to lesbians and bisexual women and had spent considerable time volunteering in gay and lesbian organizations, that she would specialize in an entirely different area of study in graduate school. She feared the effects on her career if her sexual orientation was to become known.

Sin Lee

Sin Lee spent over two months looking for housing before she found the perfect apartment for herself and her partner. She had mentioned to the landlord that she would be moving in with a roommate and the landlord indicated that he would prefer that only one person be on the lease.

Sin Lee's credit checked out and she brought her partner over to look at the apartment one more time before signing the lease. The landlord overheard them talking, figured out that they were lesbians, and told them that he would not have any "dykes" living in his building. He refused to rent them the apartment. When Sin Lee called the National Center for Lesbian Rights, she found out that in their county there was nothing they could do; the discrimination was entirely legal.

Unless lesbians, gays, and bisexuals are specifically protected by state or local laws or organizational policies, it is legal to fire them, refuse to hire or promote them, refuse them housing, or refuse them access to public accommodations. Even in those places where lesbians, gays, and bisexuals are protected against discrimination, it is expensive, emotionally taxing, and very difficult to prove discrimination based on sexual orientation. Often, when lesbians and bisexual women are the object of discrimination, other reasons are offered, making it difficult to determine the role that the discrimination plays.

In the backlash against local protective laws, several state and local governments, including Colorado, Idaho, Maine, Oregon, Washington, Cincinnati (Ohio), and Dade County (Florida), have tried to pass laws preventing local governmental bodies from protecting the rights of lesbians and gays. In a highly publicized case, Colorado succeeded, during a statewide election, in passing such an ordinance, which, when appealed to the Supreme Court in 1996, was rejected as being unconstitutional. In 1996, the federal government almost succeeded in passing legislation that would prohibit job discrimination based on sexual orientation.

≼ FAMILY LAW

――――― ℮ ―――――

Karen and Juanita

Karen and Juanita were in the eighth year of a long-term relationship. They lived in the house they had purchased together. Karen lost her job during a large company layoff and was unable to find employment. Juanita supported them, but her company offered health insurance coverage only for married couples. Karen had a preexisting mental health condition and they were unable to afford insurance for her. Karen obtained medical and mental health services only when absolutely necessary. During the entire three years while she looked for a job, she took her psychiatric medication only when she was able to afford it and did not receive any preventive medical services.

Barbara and Candid

Barbara and Candid registered their domestic partnership with the city of San Francisco two years into their relationship. Since Barbara worked for a company that offered domestic partnership benefits, Candid was able to enjoy these benefits as she worked as an independent contractor. However, Barbara paid approximately $70 a month in taxes on the value of the benefits.

Dominique and Eliza

Living together over the course of their 12-year relationship, Dominique and Eliza each had individual credit cards and bank accounts, as well as joint accounts. Neither, however, had written a will. Dominique had inherited the house from her grandmother two years before they began to live together, but when Eliza moved in, she and

Dominique shared all the household expenses including major repairs to the house. Eliza and Dominique both believed their families to be supportive of their relationship, alternating holidays between the families.

At the age of 55, Dominique was diagnosed with late stage breast cancer and died within a year. Eliza took all of her vacation time and some unpaid time off to care for and be with Dominique during the final months.

Immediately following her death, Dominique's family came to claim the house where Dominique and Eliza had lived for the past 12 years, as well as her savings and all the valuables in the house, many of which had been given to her by Dominique or they had bought together. Dominique was left not only grieving for her life partner, but without the home she had helped create and financially support. She decided that she could not afford legal recourse, emotionally or financially, and she returned to live with her family.

Darah

Darah came out as a lesbian at the age of 29 after she had already had two children with her husband. Her husband was outraged and threatened not only to sue for custody but that he would deny her any visitation with her children at all. When she told her lawyer that she planned to live with her female lover, he suggested that she would be wasting her time trying to gain custody of the children. He told her that not only would the battle be painful for her children, but that the publicity surrounding her case would negatively affect her, her partner, and her children. Darah decided not to sue for custody and agreed to limited visitation only when her partner was not around.

Marriage

Legally, the family structure in the United States consists of heterosexual parents and their children (Purcell & Hicks, 1996). The right to marriage was guaranteed as one of "fundamental importance to all individuals" as one of the "basic civil rights of man" for heterosexual couples after a Supreme Court Ruling in 1978 (Curry, Clifford, & Leonard, 1994). Legal marriage affords heterosexual couples hundreds of privileges. Ora Prochovnick conducted a search of the Westlaw legal database and found that in California alone there were over a thousand statutes dealing with legal marriages. Some of the privileges available to married couples include:

+ Filing joint income tax returns

+ Creating a marital life estate trust

+ Claiming an estate tax marital deduction

+ Claiming a family partnership tax income

+ Recovering damages based on injury to one's spouse

+ Receiving survivor's benefits

+ Visiting at hospitals, jails, and other places restricted to immediate family

+ Living in neighborhoods zoned "family only"

+ Obtaining health insurance, dental insurance, and bereavement leave as a spouse

+ Collecting unemployment when one moves with a spouse to a new location because he or she has obtained a new job

+ Getting residency status for the noncitizen spouse to avoid deportation

+ Automatically making medical decisions in cases where a spouse is injured or incapacitated

+ Automatically inheriting a spouse's property

+ Automatically receiving guardianship over children (Purcell & Hicks, 1996).

Lesbian and bisexual women do not receive any of these benefits because they cannot legally marry their female partners in the United States. Since 1971, the right for same-sex couples to marry has been challenged several times and approached in various ways. Until 1993, plaintiffs unsuccessfully sued for the constitutional right of marriage, for the constitutional right to associate, for the constitutional right to exercise their religion, and to protect against discrimination due to their sexual orientation. In 1993, the Hawaii Supreme Court ruled that denying same-sex couples the right to get married violates the state constitution. In this case, the state, which has particularly powerful constitutional clauses for sex protection, was being sued based on sex discrimination. If a woman can marry a man and not a woman, then the state is discriminating against the woman whom she wants to marry. As of this writing, Hawaii's Supreme Court found that the state could not meet the compelling interest/strict scrutiny test. The state is appealing the case and during the appeal process, same-sex couples will not be allowed to marry (Purcell & Hicks, 1996).

This case has sparked enormous debate and backlash. Several states have passed preemptive legislation so that if Hawaii legalizes same-sex marriages, they will not have to recognize these marriages in their state. The federal government also passed preemptive legislation in 1996. The Defense of Marriage Act (DOMA) specifies that, regardless of what happens in Hawaii, the privileges of legal marriage are for heterosexual couples only, and the federal government will not recognize same-sex marriages even if an individual state decides to do so. This bill also stipulates that if same-sex couples are married in one state, other states do not have to recognize the marriage legally and that the preemptive legislation that has been passed can be enforced.

The ramifications of this legislation, if enacted, are overwhelming. Couples who are married in a state where same-sex marriage is legal and then move to a state where same-sex marriage is not legal will find themselves legally unmarried. Legal scholars predict that, because the federal government has become involved in the marriage laws through DOMA, that at some point the U.S. Supreme Court will end up ruling on same-sex marriages.

Domestic Partnerships

In an attempt to mitigate some of the lack of access to the privileges that marriage provides heterosexual couples, some female couples have, in those places where it is available, elected to register as domestic partners with their county or city government and receive domestic partnership benefits through their workplace.

A domestic partnership recognizes two people (same sex or opposite sex) who are cohabiting and in a committed relationship, but who are not legally married. Typically, domestic partnership benefits allow the partner to receive health and dental benefits, bereavement leave, family sick leave, and other economic benefits. San Francisco currently allows domestic partners to participate in a civil ceremony to acknowledge their relationship and ruled that any business that has contracts with the city provide the same benefits to domestic partners that they do for married couples. Because domestic partnerships are not recognized by the state or federal government, their advantages are limited. For example, domestic partners are taxed on the estimated value of the healthcare benefits that the dependent partner receives (not true of heterosexual couples). Also, domestic partners cannot apply for green cards for their noncitizen partners. During the debate surrounding DOMA, there was talk of the possibility of a different type of marital structure for same-sex couples such as domestic partnerships, so that they could receive the same economic and social benefits, but this was excluded before the bill that was passed.

Parenting and Custody

The law does almost nothing to protect the estimated one to five million lesbians and their six to fourteen million children living in the United States today (Patterson, 1992). Although there is a growing body of scientific literature on children raised in lesbian and bisexual households, many courts continue to make custody decisions based on myths (Purcell & Hicks, 1996). These myths depict lesbians as child molesters and man-haters, incapable of raising children to become healthy adults.

Court systems claim to make their decisions in child custody cases in the "best interests of the child," a decision left totally to the discretion of the judge. Meyer (1992) describes different types of judicial analysis of the fitness of homosexual parents. Judges adhering to the *per se approach* automatically assume that homosexual households are detrimental to the child and the child should be removed.

In what Meyer calls the *middle ground approach*, it is not the identity but rather homosexual behavior that is presumed to be detrimental to the child. In these cases, the lesbian mother is often awarded custody or visitation but under strict restrictions so that the child is not exposed to homosexual behavior. Restrictions include not allowing the mother's partner to live in the household, or in some cases, even visit with the children, not allowing the lesbian mother and her partner to show any type of affection for each other in front of the children, and not permitting the children to be brought to any lesbian or bisexual event such as a gay pride parade. These limitations greatly restrict the lives of the lesbian mother, her partner, and her children.

Finally, the best chance the lesbian mother has is when the judge takes what Meyer calls the *nexus approach*, whereby homosexuality is not simply presumed to be detrimental, but rather that actual harm must be demonstrated. Several lesbian mothers have gained unrestricted custody of their children after proving (through presentation of evidence) that their lesbianism has not been detrimental to the children, calling as witnesses psychological experts familiar with the research indicating that children of lesbians are as healthy as those of heterosexual women.

Similarly, the legal system does little to protect lesbian and bisexual women who become mothers *after* coming out about their relationships with women. There are essentially four ways in which lesbians and bisexual women have children after coming out, either as single women or within a relationship with two mothers; (1) insemination (natural or artificial), (2) fostadopt (foster care placement leading to adoption) (3) international adoption, and (4) private adoptions. All of these routes are difficult and ridden with obstacles, especially for lesbians and bisexual women who disclose their sexual orientation.

Many lesbians and bisexual women who wish to have children are rejected from the two main sources which can help them through the insemination process, sperm banks and private physicians, neither of which is well regulated by federal or state governments. Both sperm banks and private physicians can choose to inseminate only "appropriate" families and often rule out single mothers and lesbians. The lesbian or bisexual woman has no legal recourse. There are women's clinics and organizations which either directly help women find sperm banks or private physicians willing to accept single mothers and/or lesbians.

Alternatively, lesbians and bisexual mothers can bypass medical intervention and use a known sperm donor and fresh sperm, but they risk other potential legal and health problems. The known biological father can sue for custody or visitation, and if he is a heterosexual married male, he has a good chance of winning. There may also be concerns about HIV/AIDS. In other cases, even though a lesbian or bisexual woman agrees to allow the biological father to play a role in the child's life, she goes on to deny visitation after the birth of the child.

It is useful for health care providers to keep abreast of the local laws about insemination procedures and the best ways to protect the biological mother, the biological father, and any other adults who will be involved in the child's life. If the health care professionals are unable or unwilling to support insemination for single or lesbian mothers, then they should recommend providers in their area who can provide this type of support.

For women who want to adopt children, there are three options; fostadopt, international adoption, and private adoptions. All options may not be available, however, since at the time of this writing, New Hampshire and Florida have laws forbidding lesbians and gay men from adopting children and/or becoming foster parents; whereas in many other states it is not law, but rather is internal policy.

To deal with these constraints, one partner will usually apply for the adoption without disclosing her sexual orientation. When the individual lies about her sexual orientation, there is little chance for a second parent adoption. Two-parent lesbian adoptions are extremely rare, except in areas such as San Francisco, where there is support for female-headed families.

As with most issues in family law, foster-adoptions depend on the location. For example, in California, it is illegal to discriminate in foster placements, including sexual orientation. However, reports may be biased against the foster placement or adoption because of the sexual orientation of the potential mothers. Often the "less desirable children" (e.g., AIDS babies, children with learning difficulties) are easier for lesbians and single mothers to adopt. The Department of Social Services (DSS) sometimes does try to place lesbian and gay foster children with lesbian and gay parents.

In foster-adoptions, usually only one of the women is granted the adoption, making two-parent adoption all but impossible. Sometimes the additional woman will try to adopt the child through a second parent adoption at a later date. Until that occurs, however, the nonadoptive mother has no legal ties to the child.

Some lesbian and bisexual women choose international adoption, but they too must hide their sexual orientation from the foreign organization since, at the time of this writing, no country will place a child with an out lesbian family. It is possible for them to be out to their social service worker in the United States, but that is risky, since it may sabotage their chances. And, as in other cases of adoption, the legal tie is only with one adoptive parent. Such adoptions are also expensive, can take a long time, require extensive travel, and often can fall through for any number of reasons, many having to do with the policies in the child's home country.

In independent adoption, a female couple searches for a woman who wants her child to be adopted, goes through the correct legal channels, and then adopts the child once it is born. Legally, this almost always takes the form of single parent adoption. In independent adoptions, it can be difficult to find a woman who is willing to have her child adopted by a female couple; even if she does agree at first, it is not uncommon for the mother to change her mind. The risk is heightened if the designated adoptive parent or the couple has not made it clear that they are lesbian. Even if those obstacles are overcome, the adoption must be approved by the Department of Social Services (DSS) with all of its inherent biases.

One of the most significant issues that arises for lesbian and bisexual women who bear or adopt children concerns the rights of the partner who is not legally or biologically the parent. In most cases, the nonbiological mother (in the case of insemination or a prior heterosexual relationship) and the mother who is not the legal adoptive mother have no standing with the child. This means that they do not even have the right to be heard by the court in a custody hearing. The woman who is the legal parent of the child can determine what access, if any, her ex-partner may have to the child. And, if the legal parent dies, then her biological family has stronger legal ties to the child than does the nonlegal parent, even if she has raised the child as a mother for the child's entire life.

Lesbian and bisexual women partners often find that it is extremely difficult to insure that there is a legal relationship between the child and both parents. In some states, a lesbian or bisexual woman can participate in a second-parent adoption, whereby as the nonbiological mother, she adopts the child and the biological mother maintains her legal rights. However, in such cases the biological father, if known, must give up or share his rights with the nonbiological mother. In addition, the second parent adoption must be demonstrated to be in the best interests of the child, something that can be extremely problematic. In order to be granted a second-parent adoption, the family must undergo scrutiny by the Department of Social Services. In some states there are friendly

DSS workers who, although they are required to make a negative recommendation because there is no marital certificate, can give a favorable report on the family. A judge hearing the case can likewise rule in favor of the adoption, based on the positive home environment. However, in other locations, second-parent adoptions are illegal or can be denied if the DSS worker submits a report biased by the mother's homosexuality.

Whatever mechanism they choose to have a child, lesbians and bisexual women fight the legal system at almost every level. Even though research has indicated that their children are as healthy and well-adjusted as those raised by their heterosexual counterparts, legal and social biases prevail. And, since custody can always be contested, lesbian and bisexual women run the constant risk of losing their children.

⊰ DEATH AND DISABILITY LAW

───────℮───────

Dana and Janet

Dana was hit by a car while riding her bicycle. In her wallet, the team in the emergency room found an emergency contact card with her partner Janet's name and work phone number. When they called, Janet rushed to see her but was told that only "immediate family" could visit and that they had already called Dana's parents. They would not even tell Janet what Dana's condition was or what her chances of survival were. Janet paced the waiting room for the next six hours until Dana's parents arrived and informed the hospital staff that the women were lifetime partners and that Janet should be considered part of the family.

Francisca and Georgia

Francisca was diagnosed with major depressive disorder at the age of 30. She met Georgia at the age of 32, just as her illness took a turn for the worse. She was hospitalized after a particularly acute suicidal episode, during which Georgia was denied visitation until Francisca was stabilized on medication two days later. After Francisca left the hospital she and Georgia went to a lawyer for help in protecting their relationship and rights in the case of another emergency.

Francisca knew that she did not want electroconvulsive shock treatment (ECT) and that she did not want to be given large doses of medicine without her consent. She also knew, in the event of a longer term hospitalization, that she wanted it to be in a facility that was closer to her partner and her social supports, not a distant one near her parents. She believed that her partner would be more able than her parents to make sure her wishes were respected. She also knew that Georgia would be able to take care of her bills and other financial obligations if she was unable to handle them herself.

Francisca and Georgia found a lawyer who drafted for both of them a living will and a durable power of attorney that would cover both health care and finances. They gave copies to Francisca's psychologist, psychiatrist, and physician, making sure that it was put both in her psychiatric and her medical records. They also kept a copy at the lawyer's office and several at home. Finally, they sent a copy to Francisca's family with a letter explaining why they made these decisions and indicated that Georgia would be talking to them about the decisions she would be making and insure that they be kept informed of any future emergencies.

Several years later, Francisca experienced another acute depressive/ suicidal episode and Georgia took her to the emergency room. They found that this time, Georgia was able to participate fully in her care and be treated as immediate family.

Laws affecting death and disability, including the terms under which property may be inherited and who can make decisions for a seriously ill or disabled spouse, have a profound effect on same-sex couples. Because they cannot marry, they do not have the same rights as married couples and must often seek extraordinary or extreme measures to protect themselves and their partners. This difference before the law has a serious impact on the health and well-being of couples as well as their children.

Legally, an unmarried woman is a child, with her closest ties to her parents. For unmarried children, if there are no living parents or adult children, then there is a legal order of relatives determining the order of connection (Ettelbrick, 1996). The lesbian's female partner is not legally connected to her at all. Janet and Dana were lucky in that Dana's parents respected their relationship and were willing to convey their support to the emergency room staff.

In many other cases, however, either the hospital or emergency room staff has refused to recognize the partner even if the patient has requested to see her and the family has supported that request. Often the family does not know about or acknowledge the relationship between the couple and will actively fight to have the partner excluded from any decision making and from visiting the incapacitated partner. In such cases, the female partner may be excluded from medical decisions about the following:

+ Treatment (e.g., whether or not to have surgery, which medications to administer, when to use extraordinary means to sustain life).

+ Providers who will treat the patient.

+ Facilities where she will be treated. (This issue is particularly important in same-sex couples when the patient's parents or adult children may want her to be treated near them, even if it means moving her away from her partner and her social supports.)

+ Visitation in the hospital and who has priority.

Medical Emergency and Death

Even though lesbians and bisexual women can take steps to protect their relationship and rights in the case of medical emergencies, there is no guarantee that the documents that they write will be respected by the courts if challenged by the woman's biological or adoptive family.

The following documents, although important for all patients, are particularly important for lesbians and bisexual women who have no legal connection to each other. If they can afford the expense, it is advisable that all papers be drawn up by attorneys, although standard forms can be obtained from the legal resources listed in Appendix A.

Legal Documents

Durable Power of Attorney for Health Care. This document allows lesbians and bisexual women to have their partners handle medical care decisions in cases where they cannot make the decisions themselves. A durable power of attorney can be as broad or as narrow as the woman wishes. It should include visitation priorities that assure that a woman's partner will be able to visit her. Additionally, it can include the power to enlist and dismiss medical personnel, to gain access to medical records and other personal information, and to obtain a court order authorizing the withholding or obtaining of medical treatment.

Medical Directive/Living Will. This document allows the individual to determine in advance what she does and does not want to be a part of her treatment. Because it clearly specifies her intentions prior to being incapacitated, these directives may be particularly important in cases where the providers are rejecting her partner. Life and death decisions, such as life support and pain relief, are usually put forth in the living will.

Conservatoryship/Guardianship. This document allows the lesbian or bisexual woman to specify that she wishes her partner to make personal and business decisions in case she is incapacitated.

Last Will and Testament. This document allows the individual to choose what happens to her property and her children in the event of her death. If a lesbian or bisexual woman has no will, then all her property and sometimes the joint property that she cannot prove is joint may go to relatives.

Revocable Living Trust. This can be a way for same-sex couples to avoid probate (court proceeding). A revocable living trust is created by establishing a trust document, giving the trust a name, and listing all of the trust property. Because the trust states that it is revocable, it can be revoked or changed at any time before the grantor dies, as long as she is mentally competent. The grantor (person setting up the trust) names the beneficiaries and the successor trustee to manage the trust after she dies. The trust is signed, notarized, and all property listed on the trust with titles must be transferred to this trust. When the woman dies, the property is transferred to the successors by the successor trustee without any court proceeding (Curry et al., 1994).

Stand-by Guardian. In some localities, courts have allowed for a stand-by guardian to be appointed by a terminally ill patient so that she knows by whom and under what circumstances her children will be cared for upon her death.

⋞ IMMIGRATION LAW

Women may find themselves in the difficult situation of falling in love with women from other countries and wanting to pursue long-term relationships with them. The severity of the battles they face, as well as the differences in their situation because of their partner's country of origin, their profession and education level, and their financial resources and familial support, are all highly significant. Adair Fox describes her story below.

———————— ℮ ————————

Shelley and Adair

"Shelley and I met at a small college in Massachusetts. She was from Toronto, while I was from Washington, D.C. . . . . In 1993 we went on a long sea kayaking vacation through Alaska and realized that we were in love. One year later, Shelley left her job in Boston to join me in San Francisco. We are currently planning a commitment ceremony. Our adventurous romance has turned into something more serious and we are beginning a stage of life that will hopefully include rewarding careers, children, a comfortable home, and a community of friends and family. . . . While I am excited for our commitment ceremony, I am also angry that our government does not recognize same-sex partnerships. The discrimination is blatant. If we were a heterosexual couple, we could get married in either Canada or the United States, thus enabling one of us to earn an unlimited right to work and live in that country and be eligible for citizenship. . . .

"So far Shelley has gotten by on year-to-year "TN visas." Every November 1st, Shelly flies to Seattle and drives a rental car about three hours to a tiny town on the border to renew her visa. Her trek is expensive and long. While she is qualified for the TN visa by most accounts, it seems there are very few immigration officers who actually understand the visa. . . . Shelley feels lucky that she finally found an informed and friendly officer at this particular border crossing. She always calls *beforehand to make sure she arrives at the office during his shift. In the meantime, I anxiously wait by the phone at home.*

"This arrangement is unsatisfactory in two major ways. First, we live with the constant worry that immigration policy in the United States or Canada will become more restrictive.

"The U.S. Immigration Act of 1990 provided for a huge increase in immigrants. . . . Under the Democratic leadership of Clinton and the Republican leadership of Congress, the immigration laws have had a somewhat confused focus. Recent reforms, including California's Proposition 187, have been more restrictive. Illegal immigrants are the biggest scapegoat today. . .

"The second and more immediate problem is that Shelley is highly discouraged by career concerns. She is eligible for this year-to-year TN visa as long as her job requires her masters' degree in Education Counseling. . . . Since Shelley wants to move out of the field of counseling, she is trapped. . ."

------------ ℮ ------------

Options for Couples with an Immigrant Partner

The Lottery. The Diversity Visa program, popularly known as "the lottery," is Congress's attempt to increase the number of Europeans immigrating to the United States. Only 50,000 are awarded each year, primarily for Europeans, although there are a few slots for people from other countries. Most couples, even those from non-European countries, try to win visas through the lottery.

Fraudulent Marriage. If the immigrant partner marries a male U.S citizen, her husband can petition for a conditional green card. She can later request the removal of her conditional status and keep her green card for life. Sometimes a lesbian couple and a gay male couple in the same predicament will marry each other's partners. Penalties for the United States citizen are up to 5 years in prison, a fine of $250,000, and the immigrant risks deportation. The Immigration and Naturalization Service conducts at least two interviews in the first 2 years of the marriage; the married couple has to exhibit a convincing married life and must demonstrate that they know the intimate details of each other's lives. They must have convinced acquaintances that they are legitimately married, as the INS reserves the right to interview neighbors, friends, employers, and relatives. The INS can make unexpected visits to the couple's home, have access to mailing lists, credit records, and IRS forms. Therefore, the couple has to be careful that the married immigrant is not traceable to any lesbian, gay, bisexual, or transgender organizations and that there is not anything indicating that they may be a part of a lesbian or bisexual couple. The stress of this fraudulent marriage "solution" is almost unbearable for the immigrant, her partner, and the man she "married." Because even after the nonconditional green card is issued, the fraudulent marriage can be uncovered and prosecuted, the couple will always live with the fear of being discovered.

Family-Based Preferences for Green Cards. If the immigrant woman has American-born children and she can prove that she has lived in the United States for 10 years, and that it would be a hardship for her to move back to her country of origin, then she can apply for a "cancellation of removal" to avoid deportation when her visa expires.

Employment-Based Preferences for Green Cards. Employment-based preferences for green cards are based on a system in which a total number of visas are given to a specific group of aliens each year. Simply put, an employer sponsors an immigrant while demonstrating that no one else is available and qualified to take her job. It typically takes between 1 and 2 years to process. However, this process is time-consuming and costly (at least $5,000 in legal fees) and limits the immigrant's job flexibility and bargaining power. It is also a solution primarily for highly educated immigrants.

Residence in the Immigrant's Native Country. There are several countries in which a U.S. citizen can obtain legal status more easily than her partner could in the U.S.

Each of these mechanisms for a citizen and a noncitizen to share their life in the United States is laden with other types of discrimination. White women do not have to contend with the racial discrimination that women of color often confront throughout the entire process. Well-educated people, especially those with jobs that are desirable in the United States, have much better chances at TN visas than those who are not as well educated or whose training in their country is not valued in the United States (e.g., midwife). All the options previously described are expensive both in time and money, not to mention worry and uncertainty.

Overall, women who are in relationships with immigrant women are under constant stress both in the present and in planning their futures. In addition, the immigrant woman may have difficulty obtaining health care, as ballot initiatives such as California's Proposition 187 deny health care and education to illegal immigrants. Some national and state governments voted to restrict access to health care and other social services, even for legal immigrants.

✍ IMPLICATIONS FOR
HEALTH PROFESSIONALS

✦ It is important that health care providers are aware of local and state laws affecting lesbians and bisexual women so they can understand patients' circumstances, the information they provide or omit, and their attitudes and behavior. Patients and colleagues should be referred to organizations that may be able to help. In some areas where discrimination is legal, fighting the legal system may be less productive than making sure patients have the support they need to deal with and accept their situation.

✦ Make sure that lesbian and bisexual patients have completed the legal documents necessary to protect themselves in the case of a medical emergency, disability, or death. Even if they are not with a partner, they may be estranged from their family and choose to designate a close friend to make or help make medical decisions. Patients can obtain the documents or referrals to lesbian and bisexual friendly lawyers through the national legal organizations.

✦ Be aware of the stress that legal battles between parents can have on their children. It may appropriate to refer both the children and their parents to counseling.

✦ Advocate for inclusion of sexual orientation and gender identity in your office's or organization's antidiscrimination clause, especially if there are no local or state ordinances in your area protecting lesbians and bisexual women. Be sure that colleagues are aware of legal concerns of lesbians and bisexual women, of available resources, and legal documents necessary to protect themselves.

✦ Be honest with yourself about how prepared you are to make decisions about the role that you are willing to play in advocating for lesbian and bisexual patients. Are you willing to inseminate lesbian mothers? Will you involve the nonbiological mother in the care of the child, even when the biological family denies her rights?

9

Parenting

—————— ❧ ——————

Jeanine

Jeanine seemed more frazzled than usual at her regular physical exam. Dr. Carrington, her physician, asked her what was causing her stress. She told him about her pending divorce and her worries about retaining custody of her two young children. Dr. Carrington, who knew Jeanine to be an excellent mother, was puzzled. Jeanine, after a long pause, told Dr. Carrington that she had fallen in love with a woman and that her lawyers told her the sodomy laws in her state could give her husband the right to take her children away from her. Dr. Carrington, taken aback by this new information, did not know how to respond. He continued with the physical exam.

Stephanie and Kathleen

Stephanie and Kathleen approached their physician, Dr. Summers, telling her they wanted to have a baby and asking her to help them. Dr. Summers asked how they intended to have the child. The two women had already decided that Stephanie would bear the child and that they would conceive through donor insemination (DI), but beyond that they were unsure of the details. Dr. Summers had never before dealt with two women wanting to have a child together, although she could only imagine the complications.

She agreed to help them with the process and advised them to find a lawyer specializing in lesbian and gay issues. In the meantime, Dr. Summers researched the subject and recommended several books and a national organization. Dr. Summers was surprised to discover that in their state, in order for the donor not to have responsibility for the child, a physician had to do the insemination. She was relieved to learn that her preconceived belief that children raised in lesbian headed homes would be at greater risk for developmental problems were unfounded. Stephanie and Kathleen joined a local lesbian and gay parenting group and were able to find a lawyer who helped them through the legal maze.

Fourteen months later, they had their first child.

Sandra and Leslie

Sandra and Leslie planned to give birth to one child apiece. Leslie was to bear the first child. Sandra fully supported this plan, although when Leslie became pregnant, Sandra experienced her first pang of jealousy. As Leslie's pregnancy progressed, Sandra felt left out of the process.

Sandra was very involved in the actual birth, but when they brought the child home, she felt like a bystander. She longed to have the bond that Leslie was establishing with the infant as she nursed her. Sandra also found that people did not know how to acknowledge her new role as a co-parent. As the tension built, Leslie and Sandra decided to seek counseling.

The therapist worked with them to develop ways in which Leslie could strengthen Sandra's relationship with the baby. They also discussed their response when people inquired about the baby's parents. As they worked in therapy on their difficulties, they began to feel like a family. They were also better prepared to deal with Leslie's feelings when Sandra became pregnant two years later.

Maxine

Maxine tried to get pregnant for more than 2 years before she decided to look into international adoptions. She located a group of parents who had adopted internationally so that she and her partner, Jay, could prepare and learn more about the process.

The first thing to become obvious was the financial commitment and emotional strain that international adoptions caused. They set up a savings account and about a year later had enough cash to start the process. They found out about several successful adoptions from an organization that worked with orphanages in Romania. They contacted the agency. Maxine was to adopt as a single mother with the hope that Jay could eventually establish legal ties to the child. They did not identify themselves as lesbians.

About 6 months after contacting the agency, they were notified that there was a baby available for adoption. Maxine went to Romania to bring the baby back, but the adoption fell through. Both Maxine and Jay were stressed, financially and emotionally.

It took months for them to again save enough money. Four months later they were contacted again, this time about a 2-year-old girl. They had said they preferred an infant, but at this point they were willing to adopt a toddler, so they readily agreed.

Maxine went to Romania a second time and instantly fell in love with the little girl. She was very small for her age, but seemed to be in reasonably good health. Maxine spent 2 months in Romania working through the many obstacles. Finally, she had the paperwork and the medical clearance.

Four years after Maxine had first tried to get pregnant, they finally had a healthy child.

Susanna

Liana and Jill had Susanna after having been together for 4 years. Liana was the biological mother, although Jill worked at home and took care of the baby.

When Susanna was seven, Liana was killed in a car accident. The courts, rather than awarding Jill custody, awarded custody to Liana's parents. Eventually, Liana's parents successfully adopted Susanna and would not allow Jill visiting privileges. Jill, having limited funds, was unable to fight the decision.

Susanna became more and more lethargic and gained a considerable amount of weight. Her pediatrician became worried about Susanna. He called Jill, knowing her financial situation, and put her in contact with a national lesbian legal association where she was able to find affordable counsel. Meanwhile, he suggested to Susanna's grandparents that they *find her a therapist to help her deal with the loss of her mothers, Lianna and Jill.*

Maria

Maria lived with her biological mother and her mother's female partner of 7 years. In her second year of high school, she decided that she could not hide any longer, and she told her best friend about her mothers.

Soon it was all over the school and she was being called "Lezzie" and other derogatory names. Her mothers visited the principal and arranged to have members of a local gay and lesbian center come to talk to the students about their own lives and conduct antihomophobia training. Although it took a while and it was painful at first, Maria's family was eventually accepted by most of the students in her classes.

Although it is impossible to determine the exact number of lesbian and bisexual women who are parents, estimates range from 1 to 5 million lesbian mothers with 6 to 14 million children (Patterson, 1992). Most lesbians and bisexual women with children had their children while in heterosexual relationships and continue to have full or partial custody after coming out as lesbians. Increasingly, lesbians and bisexual women are having children through donor insemination or adopting children while in relationships with female partners. One or both women may have legal connections to the child depending on state laws, although at this writing, two-parent adoptions by same-sex couples were rare. As the number of out lesbians and bisexual women with children increases, health professionals are more likely to encounter lesbian and bisexual parenting issues both before and after conception. It is likely that lesbian and bisexual parents will rely on health professionals to answer basic questions about their parenting concerns.

⊲⊱ LESBIANS AND BISEXUAL WOMEN AS PARENTS: COMMON THEMES

Often, when a lesbian or bisexual woman announces that she is pregnant, she is seen as selfish for bringing a child into a difficult situation. She might be asked to justify her decision. Pregnancy might not be cause for joyful celebration, especially among family or acquaintances who accept her sexual orientation, but do not approve of her becoming a parent. The mother to be will likely find that she faces as much confrontation as she does support (Pies, 1985).

Coming Out

Many lesbians, when they decide to become parents, decide to come out to their biological families, friends, and coworkers about their homosexuality and their intentions to parent. This may lead to rejection not only of the woman's decision to parent, but of her homosexuality as well. It may be helpful to plan with your lesbian or bisexual female patients, when they come to you about parenting issues, the best ways to come out so that she and her child have the best chance for acceptance.

Decisions

Female couples, unless they have children from a previous relationship with a man, have many decisions to make when having children. There are many questions to be answered when considering birth and adoption.

Birth

If a couple, who will be the mother? The father? Will the father be a known donor? Unknown? Known at 18 at the child's request? What role will the father have in the child's life? How will the insemination take place? Through a sperm bank? Through a physician? Privately?

Adoption

What type of adoption? International? Private? Foster child? Are they willing to adopt a toddler or older child? A child with disabilities? A child of a different race or ethnicity? If they adopt internationally, from what country? Through an agency or privately? Which mother will adopt the child? Will they be open about their lesbianism?

General Parenting

Overall, parenting for women who are in relationships with women is overwhelmingly complex. Dealing with social, personal, and medical complexities can be highly stressful for the mothers and the children and requires parents to think carefully about every aspect of the parenting process. The more the health care providers understand these concerns and issues, the better able they will be to advise and provide care for their patients who are lesbian parents and for their children.

⊰ CHILDREN OF LESBIAN PARENTS

Research

Part of the disapproval that lesbian mothers face stems from the assumption that they are inferior parents and that their children will face permanent personal and developmental problems. Research, comparing the children of lesbian mothers to those of heterosexual mothers, has shown that children of lesbians are not significantly different from those raised by heterosexual parents (Patterson, 1992). It is important to note that this research primarily targets children from white, middle-class families and that the mothers were typically previously married and then embraced a lesbian identity.

Specifically, as cited in Patterson's (1992) comprehensive review of the literature, Kirkpatrick, Smith, & Roy (1981) found that there was no difference in terms of the gender identity between the children of heterosexual single mothers and the children of lesbians. Kirkpatrick et al. found no difference in sex role behavior. Golombok, Spencer, & Rotter (1983) and Huggins (1989) found no difference in sexual orientation and Paul (1986) and Gottman (1990) found that the percentage of lesbian and gay children of lesbian mothers was within "normal" limits. Golombok et al. (1983) found no difference in behavioral or emotional problems. Gottman (1990) found that adult daughters of lesbians when compared to those of heterosexuals were not significantly different on 17 scales of psychological adjustment and rated more favorably on one. Puryear (1983) and Huggins (1989) found that there was no difference in self-concept. Puryear (1983) found that there was no difference in locals of control and Green, Mandel, Hotvedt, Gray, & Smith (1986) found that there was no difference in results on intelligence tests. Green et al. (1986) found that there was no difference in popularity, Golombok et al. (1983) found that there was no difference in the ability to maintain social relationships, and Kirkpatrick et al. found that in lesbian-headed households the mothers were more concerned about insuring that their children had adult males in their lives and Golombok et al. found that the children in lesbian households had more contact with their fathers.

More recently, Golombok & Tasker (1996) found in their longitudinal study that adult children of lesbian families were more likely to experiment with people of the same sex, but that the large majority of children who grew up in lesbian homes identified as heterosexual. Flaks, Ficher, Masterpasqua, & Joseph (1995) found that the cognitive functioning and behavioral adjustment were not significantly different for children of lesbians than they were for children of heterosexual mothers. Similarly, the parenting skills and relationship qualities of the lesbian couples did not differ from those of the heterosexual couples.

Although none of the literature supports the claims that lesbians are inferior parents, courts continue to take children away from their lesbian mothers when the mothers disclose this information about themselves. Many lesbian mothers live in fear that this information will become known.

It is interesting to note that one research question that is often stressed when evaluating lesbian parenting, is whether the children of lesbians and bisexual women are more likely to be lesbian or gay than the children of their heterosexual counterparts. There is the automatic assumption that being lesbian is something to be avoided. There is also the assumption that if there are higher percentages of lesbianism that this is due to bad parenting rather than the genetic predisposition to being lesbian or gay.

✄ WORKING WITH LESBIAN PARENTS AND THEIR CHILDREN

Recently, Ellen Perrin and Heidi Kulkin (1996) conducted a national study to determine how well lesbian and gay parents and their children were being cared for in the health care system. They found that a large majority had had positive experiences. Indications of positive care included; maintaining eye contact with both parents, referring to both mothers as parents, showing an interest in lesbian parenting by asking for resources, acknowledging potentially stigmatizing situations, and offering to help with special issues as they arose.

On the other hand, 33% reported problems specifically related to their sexual orientation. Problems included; a lack of understanding or acceptance of same-sex parents, the need to continuously explain their family structure, and the exclusion of the nonbiological parent from emergency care.

✄ IMPLICATIONS FOR HEALTH PROFESSIONALS

+ As with any care involving lesbians and bisexual women, respect and communication are critical.

+ Forms and histories should allow for diverse family structures.

+ Books, magazines, posters, and educational material should reflect diverse family structures.

+ Providers should recognize potentially stressful situations prior to and after the children are born or adopted. They should address these issues with the parents and their children when appropriate.

❧ Conclusion

*I*t is the author's hope that the readers are now aware that lesbians and bisexual women have unique health care needs. Awareness can make a tremendous difference for these women. A few points warrant repetition. First, language and other forms of communication are critical in working with lesbians and bisexual women. Becoming aware of one's own use of language and gender specific pronouns, and the format of questions and making sure that the language used is appropriate for everyone, can open the doors to communication.

Lesbians and bisexual women are not protected in the same way as heterosexual married couples. Encouraging lesbians and bisexual women to protect themselves through appropriate legal documents is critical.

Lesbians and bisexual women are at risk for a host of behaviors and mental health symptoms due to the stress of living in a heterosexual world. Sensitivity to both external and internal homophobia and support in helping them find the support that they need both from the lesbian community and health care providers can make a tremendous difference.

Finally, lesbians and bisexual women come from all racial, ethnic, religious, and other cultural groups. It is important to think about them in all of their diversity.

ↁ Appendix A
Annotated Bibliography

he following is an annotated bibliography of books, publications, websites, and a few key journal articles. Each is on the list because it is recommended for health professionals who wish to learn more about the health and culture of their lesbian, bisexual, and transgender patients, and so that they have resources to recommend to these women. For some topics, the author has included all the references that were readily available, whereas for other topics, there was a wealth of resources from which to choose. Also included are the phone numbers as of January 1, 1998, of small presses that publish gay and lesbian material so that these more obscure books are accessible and so that it is possible to receive regular catalogs. Finally, there are the phone numbers and addresses of several bookstores through which many of these materials can be ordered.

As discussed in Chapter 8, many lesbians and bisexual women who are also from other minority groups feel isolated and invisible within the larger lesbian and bisexual women's community, the other communities to which they belong, and the mainstream. They often struggle with multiple identities and multiple oppressions, both from within the lesbian and bisexual community as well as from their other communities. Writings by women with whom they can identify may help them in their struggles to learn more about their communities and themselves. These readings are also important for health professionals who work with women from diverse backgrounds as they gain a better understanding of lesbian and bisexual women.

One way many lesbians and bisexual women tell their stories is through cultural anthologies. Typically, these edited anthologies consist of poetry, short stories, biographical accounts, photographs, and sometimes, theoretical works compiled around a particular theme (i.e., youth, ethnic and racial minorities). Other women choose to tell their own stories through full-length biographies written with or without the help of a coauthor. Still others choose to tell stories through novels based on the reality of their lives.

Some authors tell the stories of lesbian and bisexual women through oral histories and interviews. Although these stories are often not in the individual's own words, the authors of these books tell coherent stories and place the stories in context with relevant historical and sociocultural information.

Also important to understanding the health of lesbians and bisexual women are informational pieces such as full-length books and edited volumes. Included are the results of research, descriptions of programs, and the experiences of experts. These books and edited volumes are usually arranged around a particular group of people (i.e., the elderly) or a specific health issue (i.e., domestic violence).

Especially significant for health professionals are books on sexuality. Many health professionals are uncomfortable talking about sexuality with their patients or know little about lesbian sexuality. These books not only provide extensive information about a wide variety of sexual behaviors, but they also include stories, fantasies, and theoretical debates which may help the provider become accustomed to seeing the language that is used and the graphic descriptions which may help them be more comfortable when dealing with the sexuality of their lesbian and bisexual patients.

BOOKS

Lesbians and Bisexual Women of Color—General

Anthologies

Moraga, Cherríe, and Anzaldua, Gloria (1983). *This Bridge Called My Back: Writings of Radical Women of Color*. New York, NY: Kitchen Table Women of Color Press. A classic collection of poems, stories, and essays written by and for women of color. Still one of the best.

Silvera, Makeda (1991). *Piece of My Heart: A Lesbian of Colour Anthology*. Toronto, Ontario: Sister Vision Press. If someone had to choose one anthology to read in trying to better understand the concerns and lives of lesbians of color, this would be my top recommendation. The contributors are diverse, as are their styles of writing and the topics they write about. There are several pieces directly addressing health issues.

African American/Black

Anthologies

Mason-John, Valerie (1995). *Talking Black: Lesbians of African and Asian Descent Speak Out*. New York, NY: Cassell.

McKinley, Catherine, and Delaney, L. Joyce (Eds.). (1995). *Afrekete: An Anthology of Black Lesbian Writing*. New York, NY: Doubleday.

Both of these anthologies contain poems, short stories, narratives, informational pieces, and essays.

Novels

Harris, E. Lynn (1991). *Invisible Life*. New York, NY: Anchor Books.

Harris, E. Lynn (1994). *Just As I Am*. New York, NY: Anchor Books.

Harris, E. Lynn (1996). *This Too Shall Pass*. New York, NY: Anchor Books.

These novels explore the lives of the African American gay, lesbian, and bisexual communities. Highly recommended.

Native American/Two Spirited

Anthologies

Roscoe, Will (Ed.). (1988). *Living the Spirit: A Gay American Indian Anthology*. New York, NY: St. Martin's Press. The only anthology I was able to find focusing on the lives of gay American Indians.

Latina/Hispanic

Anthologies

Ramos, Juanita (1994). *Compañeras: Latina Lesbians: An Anthology*. New York, NY: Routledge. The contributors and the writing styles found in this anthology are very diverse.

Novels

de la Pea, Terri (1992). *Margins*. Seattle, WA: Seal Press.
de la Pea, Terri (1994). *Latin Satins*. Seattle, WA: Seal Press.

Two of my favorite novels depicting the lives of Latina lesbians.

Asian American/Pacific Islander

Anthologies

Lim-Hing, Sharon (Ed.). (1994). *The Very Inside: An Anthology of Writing by Asian and Pacific Islander Lesbian and Bisexual Women*. Toronto, Ontario: Sister Vision.
Mason-John, Valerie (Ed.). (1995). *Talking Black: Lesbians of African and Asian Descent Speak Out*. New York, NY: Cassell.
Ratti, Rakesh (Ed.). (1993). *A Lotus of Another Color: An Unfolding of the South Asian Gay and Lesbian Experience*. Boston, MA: Alyson Publications.

These anthologies contain poetry, short stories, essays, and narratives exploring the lives of Asian and Pacific Islander lesbians and bisexual women.

International

Anthologies

Penelope, Julia, and Valentine, Sarah (Eds.). (1990). *Finding the Lesbians: Personal Accounts From Around the World*. Freedom, CA: The Crossing Press. A unique anthology exploring the lives of lesbians from within the U.S. and beyond.

Edited Volumes

Rosenbloom, Rachel (Ed.). (1995). *Unspoken Rules: Sexual Orientation and Women's Rights*. San Francisco, CA: International Gay and Lesbian Human Rights Commission. Provides information about laws, policies, attitudes, health issues, education, etc. of lesbians and bisexual women from over two dozen countries around the world.

Disabilities

Anthologies

Luczak, Raymond (Ed.). (1993). *Eyes of Desire: A Deaf Gay and Lesbian Reader.* Boston, MA: Alyson Publications.

Tremain, Shelley (Ed.). (1996). *Pushing the Limits: Disabled Dykes Produce Culture.* Toronto, Ontario: Women's Educational Press.

Both of these anthologies are extremely helpful in understanding the lives of disabled lesbians and bisexual women. Highly recommended as references for disabled women.

Biography

Thompson, Karen, and Andrzejewski, Julie (1988). *Why Can't Sharon Kowalski Come Home.* San Francisco, CA: Spinsters/Aunt Lute. This is the story of perhaps the most notorious and visible injustice by the medical and legal systems toward a lesbian couple. Sharon Kowalski, long-term partner of Karen Thompson, was disabled in a car accident. Her parents, upon learning of the nature of Karen and Sharon's relationship obtained legal guardianship and restricted Karen from visiting her long-term partner. It was not until years later that Karen was able to be with her partner. This book is a real eye opener about the injustices that can potentially effect both same-sex partners and the disabled. It emphasizes the importance of preparing appropriate documentation for same sex partners in order to protect themselves from similar situations.

Youth

Anthologies

Grima, Tony (Ed.). (1994). *Not the Only One: Lesbian and Gay Fiction for Teens.* Boston, MA: Alyson Publications. Very accessible for teens and those who wish to understand their lives.

Singer, Bennett, L. (Ed.). (1994). *Growing Up Gay/Growing Up Lesbian: A Literary Anthology.* New York, NY: The New Press. This is a compilation of literature for youth. Consists of some new pieces written for youth from well-known gays and lesbians (i.e., Martina Navratilova) and some excerpts from works either for or about lesbians and gays. Highly recommended for

young people who are exploring their sexuality. It has an extensive resource list.

Interviews/Case Studies

Aarons, Leroy (1995). *Prayers for Bobby: A Mother's Coming to Terms with the
Suicide of her Gay Son*. San Francisco, CA: Harper San Francisco. Bobby
Griffith jumped off a bridge to his death after agonizing over his sexual
orientation. This nonfiction book portrays the anguish of Bobby's mother
as she comes to terms with her role and the role of her religion in the death
of her son. An important story that will most certainly aid in the understanding of the difficulties of coming out, particularly in a religious family.
Due, Linnea (1995). *Joining the Tribe: Growing Up Gay and Lesbian in the '90s*. New
York, NY: Anchor Books. In this book, the stories of a diverse selection of
young lesbians and gay men are told through one coherent voice. Linnea
Due provides focuses both on the stories of these young people and the
environment within which they live. Although, unlike other anthologies,
this book is not told through the actual voices of the youth, it is extremely
compelling and highly recommended for youth gay and straight, their
families, and for health professionals.
Herdt, Gilbert, and Boxer, Andrew (1993). *Children of the Horizons: How Gay and
Lesbian Teens Are Leading a New Way Out of the Closet*. Boston, MA: Beacon
Press. This full-length book is the case study of a gay and lesbian youth
organization in Chicago. Captures the complexity of the issues confronting
these youth and those who work with them.

Informational Books

Pollack, Rachel, and Schwartz, Cheryl (1995). *The Journey Out: A Guide For and
About Lesbian, Gay and Bisexual Teens*. New York, NY: Puffin Books. This
informational book is highly accessible to the teenager who wishes to learn
more about sexual minorities. The resource list is extensive.

Elderly and Middle Aged

Edited Volumes

Adleman, Jeanne, et al. (Eds.). (1993). *Lambda Gray: A Practical, Emotional, and
Spiritual Guide for Gays and Lesbians Who Are Growing Older*. North Hollywood, CA: New Castle Publishing. Included are personal reflections and

informative articles. Perhaps most useful is the extensive annotated resource and reference list.

Lee, John Alan (Ed.). (1991). *Gay Midlife and Maturity*. Binghamton, NY: Harrington Park Press. It was also published as the special edition of a
peer-reviewed journal. John Alan Lee compiled an assortment of articles
including research studies, personal experiences, and potential solutions.
One of the few compilations of work on midlife and elderly lesbians and
gays.

Sang, Barbara; Warshow, Joyce; and Smith, Adrienne (Eds.). (1991). *Lesbians at
Midlife: The Creative Transition*. San Francisco, CA: Spinsters Ink. Midlife is
a difficult transition for women in the best of circumstances and becomes
even more difficult for women in minority groups. This book is filled with
personal stories and informational articles for lesbians who have or who
are undergoing this transition.

Informational Books

Macdonald, Barbara, and Rich, Cynthia (1984). *Look Me in the Eye: Old Women,
Aging and Ageism*. San Francisco, CA: Spinsters Ink. Barbara Macdonald
and her younger lover, Cynthia Rich, write essays about ageism, particularly in the lesbian community. An extremely powerful reminder for all of
us who inadvertently treat the elderly with less respect than they deserve.
Also important for elderly women who rarely see themselves represented
in print.

Bisexuality

Anthologies

Tucker, Naomi (Ed.). (1995). *Bisexual Politics: Theories, Queries, and Visions*. New
York, NY: Harrington Park Press.

Weise, Elizabeth (Ed.). (1992). *Closer to Home: Bisexuality and Feminism*. Seattle,
WA: Seal Press.

These anthologies contain creative writing and theory.

Informational Books

Weinberg, Martin; Williams, Collin; and Pryor, Douglas (1994). *Dual Attraction:
Understanding Bisexuality*. New York, NY: Oxford University Press. Using
fieldwork, research, and surveys of 800 bisexual, gay and lesbian and

heterosexual residents of San Francisco, Weinberg, Williams, and Douglas have put forth an extensive portrayal of the complexity of bisexuality. Specifically, they describe the lives of bisexuals; they compare bisexuals, heterosexuals, and homosexuals; and they discuss the relationship between bisexuality and HIV/AIDs.

Gender Issues

Interviews

Devor, Holly (1989). *Gender Blending: Confronting the Limits of Duality.* Bloomington, IN: Indiana University Press. This book is a discussion of gender using 15 interviews of women with a variety of gender presentations. Recommended for those who are interested in exploring gender diversity.

Informational Books

Bornstein, Kate (1994). *Gender Outlaw: On Men, Women, and the Rest of Us.* New York, NY: Routledge Press. Kate Bornstein, through personal stories, interspersed with informational pieces, tells the tale of her transformation from a man to a woman, capturing the role that gender played in her life and in society.

Mackenzie, Gordene Olga (1994). *Transgender Nation.* Bowling Green, OH: Bowling Green State University Popular Press. This book explores gender diversity with an emphasis on the transsexual. It begins by discussing transgenderism within a sociological and historical context. It moves into discussing the "medicalization of transsexualism and genderism." Then you find images of transsexuals and transgenders in American popular culture complete with photographs. Finally, you will find a discussion of the gender movement. The bibliography of works cited in the end of the book can be a helpful resource in and of their own.

Novels

Feinberg, Leslie (1993). *Stone Butch Blues.* Ithaca, NY: Firebrand Books. This emotional novel portrays the life of a woman trying to grow up between the genders in the 1950s. One of my highest recommendations for those who are interested in the lives of butch women and their femme counterparts and the complexities of gender diversity.

Narratives

Pratt, Minnie Bruce (1995). *S/HE*. Ithaca, NY: Firebrand Books. Minnie Bruce Pratt, in her poetic narrative style, opens the doors to the complexity of gender in her own life and the lives of those she loves.

Socioeconomic Class

Anthologies

Penelope, Julia (Ed.). (1994). *Out of the Class Closet: Lesbians Speak*. Freedom, CA: Crossing Press. Lesbians, like all other communities, represent a diversity of classes from the very rich to those seeking survival on the streets. *Out of the Class Closet* is an admirable collection of essays addressing the complexity of class within the lesbian community. A highly recommended reading for those who want to learn about lesbians who are not typically represented in other work.

Religion

Anthologies

Spahr, Jane Adams; Poethig, Kathryn; Berry, Selisse; and McLain, Melinda (Eds.). (1995). *Called Out: The Voices and Gifts of Lesbian, Gay, Bisexual, and Transgendered Presbyterians*. Gaithersburg, MD: Chi Rho Press.

Informational Books

Shokeid, Moshe (1995). *A Gay Synagogue in New York*. New York, NY: Columbia University Press. This book details the history and daily goings on of a gay synagogue in New York. Important reading for lesbian and bisexual women trying to integrate their sexual orientation and their Jewish affiliation and heritage.

History and Politics

Oral Histories and Informational Books

Duberman, Martin (1993). *Stonewall*. New York, NY: Dutton. Duberman describes in detail the events surrounding the Stonewall Rebellion of 1969 by tracing the lives of six diverse individuals and the historical context within which they lived. An important contribution in understanding the beginning of the gay, lesbian, bisexual, and transgender rights movement as well as the lives of those who lived during this era.

Jennings, Kevin (1994). *Becoming Visible: A Reader in Gay and Lesbian History for High School and College Students*. Boston, MA: Alyson Publications. It is extremely important for young people (as well as their older counterparts) to have a sense of their culture and their history. This is the best book I've found that traces gay and lesbian history in an accessible and interesting way. Filled with passages from other readings, discussions by the editor, and questions that arise from the readings and the discussions. Recommended not only for students, but for adults as well.

Marcus, Eric (1992). *Making History: The Struggle for Gay and Lesbian Equal Rights*. New York, NY: HarperCollins. Eric Marcus, through extensive oral histories, portrays the lives of some of the most important people to the lesbian, gay, bisexual, and transgendered movement. A wonderful introduction to the history of this population for lesbians, gays, bisexuals, and transgendered people and those who are trying to learn more about them.

Vaid, Urvashi (1995). *Virtual Equality: The Mainstreaming of Gay and Lesbian Liberation*. New York, NY: Doubleday. Urvashi Vaid in this thought-provoking book discusses the politics of the lesbian and gay community. Very informative for anyone who wants to better understand lesbian and gay history and what the lesbian and gay movement is all about.

Homophobia

Edited Volumes

Blumenfeld, Warren (1992). *Homophobia: How We All Pay the Price*. Boston, MA: Beacon Press. This book provides insights about homosexuality and homophobia from a variety of perspectives including gay and lesbian people, their families, and other heterosexuals responding to the negative effects that homophobia has on society. The focus on the relevance of homophobia for heterosexuals makes it particularly useful for health professionals who want to clarify how these issues affect themselves and their practices.

Herek, Gregory, and Berril, Kevin (Eds.). (1992). *Hate Crimes: Confronting Violence Against Lesbians and Gay Men*. Newbury Park, CA: Sage Publications. This edited volume varies widely in its content from conceptual articles about the causes of heterosexism to national statistics on hate crimes. A good source for anyone interested in learning more about not only hate crimes, but homophobia and heterosexism as well.

Oikowa, M.; Falconer, D.; and Decter, A. (1994). *Resist: Essays Against a Homophobic Culture*. Toronto, Canada: Women's Educational Press.

Oikawa, M.; Falconer, D.; Elwin, R.; and Decter, A. (1993). *Outrage: Dykes and Bisexuals Resist Homophobia*. Toronto, Canada: Women's Eductaional Press.

These two volumes, one containing essays and one containing poetry and short stories, are perhaps my favorite collection of works on homophobia. They provide the reader with a comprehensive sense of the effects of homophobia and the extent to which homophobia penetrates all aspects of the lives of lesbians and bisexual women, including several essays and short stories directly addressing health issues such as HIV/AIDs and breast cancer. Highly recommended for health professionals and their lesbian and bisexual patients.

Full Length

Brenner, Claudia (1995). *Eight Bullets: One Woman's Story of Surviving Anti-Gay Violence*. Ithaca, NY: Firebrand Books. Claudia Brenner and her partner, while camping on the Appalachian Trail in Pennsylvania were shot eight times in a homophobic attack. Claudia's partner died and she was severely injured. This book describes in graphic detail the attack, her attacker's trial, and Claudia's recovery. It highlights the extent to which hate violence effects the lives of lesbians and bisexual women. An important reading for anyone who works with those who have been or has been himself, a victim of hate violence.

Domestic Violence

Edited Volumes

Lobel, Kerry (Ed.). (1986). *Naming the Violence: Speaking Out About Lesbian Battering*. Seattle, WA: Seal Press. This edited volume contains informational pieces and most importantly, the experiences of those who have survived same-sex domestic violence. Highly recommended for perpetrators and survivors and for all health professionals.

Renzetti, Claire (1992). *Violent Betrayal: Partner Abuse in Lesbian Relationships*. Newbury Park, CA: Sage Publications. This book summarizes the results of a study that Claire Renzetti conducted on same-sex domestic violence as well as additional information useful for survivors of domestic violence and health professionals who work with them. Complete with an extensive resource list.

Renzetti, Claire, and Miley, Charles (1996). *Violence in Lesbian and Gay Partnerships*. Domestic violence is typically thought of as occurring between heterosexual couples; in fact, most theories explaining domestic violence have patriarchy at their core. However, same-sex domestic violence requires a new theoretical understanding of domestic violence as well as treatments for both the perpetrator and the victim. This edited volume introduces both a theoretical and practical look at same-sex domestic violence. Perhaps most useful are the articles specifically addressing service provision for perpetrators and victims of same-sex domestic violence. Also noteworthy are the articles on the issues of same-sex violence for people of color.

Parenting

Anthologies

Arnup, Katherine (Ed.). (1995). *Lesbian Parenting: Living with Pride and Prejudice*. Charlottetown, Canada: gynergy books. Katherine Arnup has compiled an incredible diversity of emotionally charged stories of lesbians talking about their experiences having, adopting, and and in some cases not being able to have children. An important book for lesbians who are thinking about having children, those who already have them, and their health care providers.

Informational Books

Benkov, Laura (1994). *Reinventing the Family: The Emerging Story of Lesbian and Gay Parents*. New York, NY: Crown Publishers. Using interviews from gay and lesbian families, research, and legal cases, Dr. Benkov describes many issues relevant to the lesbian and gay family. She includes the experiences of both the parents and their children. The book is comprehensive and readable.

Pies, Cheri (1988). *Considering Parenthood*. San Francisco, CA: Spinsters/Aunt Lute. This workbook is a must for women considering having children with their female partners. There are discussions of the tremendous complexity of bringing children into nontraditional families with exercises and provocative questions that allow each individual to think about and make the best decisions for their personal situation. It is also tremendously useful for the provider who is guiding these women.

Substance Use

Anthologies

Swallow, Jean (Ed.). (1994). *The Next Step: Lesbians in Long-Term Recovery*. Boston, MA: Alyson Publications. This accumulation of personal accounts provides a better understanding of the experiences of lesbians in long-term recovery from addiction. It can be helpful for the individual addict and her family in gaining support as she recovers, as well as for the provider who is attempting to better understand her.

Sexuality and Relationships

Informational Books

Califia, Pat (1988). *Sapphistry: The Book of Lesbian Sexuality*. Tallahassee, FL: Naid Press. This book is one of the first comprehensive books discussing lesbian sexuality from a positive perspective and remains an important source-book for lesbians, bisexuals, and those who want to understand them better. The diversity of topics range from masturbation and fantasy to the sexuality of disabled lesbians.

Loulan, JoAnn (1990). *The Lesbian Erotic Dance: Butch Femme Androgyny and Other Rhythms*. San Francisco, CA: Spinsters Ink. This book is highly recommended for those interested in understanding butch/femme/androgyny and the way that these sexual diversities play out in the lesbian community. The book is based on case studies and a survey of 589 lesbians. It is a particularly interesting read.

Schramm-Evans, Zoe (1995). *Making Out: The Book of Lesbian Sex and Sexuality*. London, England: Pandora. This book, with beautiful photographs, is very accessible for the layperson and the health professional interested in learning about lesbian and bisexual sexuality. Includes specific health related topics (i.e., sexually transmitted diseases). Normalizes all types of sexual play. Highly recommended for health professionals to recommend to their lesbian and bisexual patients.

Tessina, Tina (1989). *Gay Relationships: How to Find Them: How to Improve Them: How to Make Them Last*. New York, NY: G.P. Putnam's Sons. A great book for those trying to understand the unique dynamics of gay relationships (as well as the dynamics that are similar to heterosexual relationships). Accessible to providers and their patients.

Edited Volumes

Califia, Pat, and Sweeney, Robin (1996). *The Second Coming: A Leatherdyke Reader*. Los Angeles, CA: Alyson Publications. This collection of informational articles about safety and what S/M parties are really like, erotic stories and poetry, pieces about the diversity of the S/M community, S/M theory, and historical articles is a must read for anyone interested in S/M. It is also an important read for anyone who may work with people who practice S/M, whether they identify with the community or not (for any health professional).

Nestle, Joan (Ed.). (1992). *The Persistent Desire: A Femme-Butch Reader*. Boston, MA: Alyson Publications. This compilation of narratives, short stories, poetry, interviews, and informational pieces may help both members from within the lesbian and bisexual community and those trying to learn more about them to understand the complexity of the butch/femme dichotomy. Also adds to the reader's sense of the history of the lesbian and bisexual women's community.

SAMOIS (1987), *Coming to Power: Writings and Graphics on Lesbian S/M*. Boston, MA: Alyson Publications. This collection not only includes erotic stories, but informational pieces on safety, the history of the S/M community in San Francisco, and some of the codes used by this community. Although this book is still recommended for those particularly interested in the S/M community, I would recommend trying to obtain the sequel first (see below).

Lesbian and Bisexual Women's Health—General

Personal Narrative

Butler, Sandra, and Rosenblum, Barbara (1991). *Cancer in Two Voices*. A female couple maps out their experience with breast cancer illness. From the perspectives of Barbara, the woman with cancer and her partner Sandra.

Edited Volumes

Cabaj, Robert, and Stein, Terry (Eds.). (1996). *Textbook of Homosexuality and Mental Health*. Washington, D.C.: American Psychiatric Press. (See mental health.)

Peterson, K. Jean (Ed.). (1996). *Health Care for Lesbians and Gay Men: Confronting Homophobia and Heterosexism*. New York, NY: Harrington Park Press. This collection of articles was simultaneously published as a special issue of the *Journal of Gay and Lesbian Social Services*. Included are articles on homophobia, youth, gay men and lesbians and the health care system, reproductive issues for lesbians, substance abuse, elderly, and legal issues.

Stern, Phyllis (Ed.). (1992). *Lesbian Health: What Are the Issues?* Washington, DC: Taylor and Francis. This collection, originally published as a special issue of *Health Care for Women International* has a diversity of peer-reviewed articles ranging from the results of studies to the description of a parenting project. Particularly noteworthy is the literature review of health care research by Patricia Stevens.

White, J. and Martinez, M. (Eds.). (1997). *The Lesbian Health Book*. A compilation of pieces from personal narratives to historical overviews. A great resource for the lesbian and her health care provider.

Mental Health

Edited Volumes

Cabaj, Robert, and Stein, Terry (Eds.). (1996). *Textbook of Homosexuality and Mental Health*. Washington, D.C.: American Psychiatric Press. This 978-page book is highly recommended not only for the mental health professional, but for everyone in the health field and anyone else who is interested in learning about lesbians and gays and to a lesser extent, bisexuals and transgendered people. Chapters include the results of research, informational articles, descriptions of theories, discussions of ethical concerns, etc. Topics include the history of treatment for gays and lesbians, the essentialist/social constructionist debate, homophobia/heterosexism, identity development, families, psychotherapy, the concerns of people of color, youth, elderly, training health professionals, and sexuality. This book is well worth the investment.

Garnets, Linda, and Kimmel, Douglas (Eds.). (1993). *Psychological Perspectives on the Lesbian and Gay Male Experiences*. New York, NY: Columbia University Press.

Greene, Beverly, and Herek, Gregory (Eds.). (1994). *Lesbian and Gay Psychology: Theory Research and Clinical Applications.* Thousand Oaks, CA: Sage Publications.

The two volumes listed above are compilations of theory, the results of research and informational articles pertaining to the lives of lesbians and gay men. They both are written for the mental health professional, although they can be useful for anyone who wishes to understand the lives of this population.

Informational Books

Kitzinger, Celia, and Perkins, Rachel (1993). *Changing Our Minds: Lesbian Feminism and Psychology.* New York, NY: New York University Press. A controversial look at the role of mental health illness and therapy in the lesbian community. Highly recommended for all mental health professionals working with this population.

Workplace

Informational Books

Winfield, Liz, and Spielman, Susan (1995). *Straight Talk About Gays in the Workplace: Creating an Inclusive, Productive Environment for Everyone in Your Organization.* New York, NY: AMACOM. Liz Winfield and Susan Spielman present not only the problems, with examples of homophobia and heterosexism in the workplace, but solutions for resolving some of the complicated issues such as delivering education, domestic partnership benefits, and the complexities of HIV/AIDS. Their step-by-step approach makes the book particularly accessible and has the potential to help make any clinic or office more friendly to lesbians and bisexual women.

Legal Issues

Informational Books

Curry, Hayden; Clifford, Denis; and Leonard, Robin (1994). *A Legal Guide for Lesbian and Gay Couples.* Berkeley, CA: Nolo Press. This guide is critical for people who are in relationships with members of the same sex as well as their health professionals. It provides critical information so that they can protect themselves and their relationships prior to emergencies. Included are forms and resource lists for further assistance. Call Nolo Press for the most updated copy. (510) 549-1976.

Hunter, Nan; Michaelson, Sherryl; and Stoddard, Thomas (1992). *The Rights of Lesbians and Gay Men: Third Edition*. Carbondale, IL: Southern Illinois University Press. A handbook of the legal concerns of lesbians and gay men. Topics include freedom of speech and association, employment, security clearances, the armed services, housing and public accommodations, family issues, criminal law, and the rights of people with HIV disease. Readable for the lesbian, gay, or bisexual individual and for those who work with them.

For Family and Friends of Gays, Lesbians, Bisexuals and Transgendered People

Informational Books

Powers, Bob, and Ellis, Alan (1996). *A Family and Friend's Guide to Sexual Orientation*. New York, NY: Routledge. Bob Powers and Alan Ellis have compiled a vast array of the stories of lesbians and gays integrated with information about these communities making this book helpful for anyone wishing to know more about lesbians and gays from their own personal perspectives.

✄ PUBLICATIONS

Academic and/or for Health Professionals (Peer Reviewed)

Journal of Homosexuality. Published by Haworth Press. 1-800-342-9678. Contains results of research, theoretical articles, book reviews, and informational articles. Many articles are about particular cultural groups or health issues. Back issues are available as well as special issues that have been released as books. Highly recommended for anyone who is interested in homosexuality.

Journal of Gay and Lesbian Psychotherapy. Published by Haworth Medical Press. 1-800-342-9678. Contains case studies, results of research, and informational articles. Very practical. Particularly useful for mental health professionals.

Journal of Gay and Lesbian Social Services. Published by Haworth Press. 1-800-342-9678. Contains results of research, informational articles, and reports from programs targeted to the social service provider. Back issues and special issues released as books are available. Highly recommended for the health professional.

Journal of the Gay and Lesbian Medical Association. Published by Plenum Publishing. 1-800-221-9369.

Magazines

Curve (formerly *Deneuve*)
(818) 760-8983
Lesbian and bisexual women's news, columns, book and record reviews.

Genre
(800) 576-9933
Gay and lesbian nonfiction, travel, news, gay life.

Off Our Backs
(202) 234-8072
Lesbian news and commentary. Includes book and record reviews and conference coverage.

On Our Backs
(415) 861-4723
Lesbian fiction and nonfiction erotica and news.

Out
(800) 876-1199
Gay and lesbian news magazine.

Sinister Wisdom
P.O. Box 3252 Berkeley, CA 94703
Lesbian fiction and nonfiction, poetry, erotica, book reviews, art, politics, and history.

Sojourner: The Women's Forum
(617) 542-0415
Women's fiction, nonfiction, poetry, news, and reviews from a feminist perspective.

10 Percent
(415) 905-8590
Lesbian and gay news and culture.

The Advocate
Lesbian and gay news coverage.
Includes entertainment reviews, gossip, editorials and columns.

Selected Presses

Alyson Publications
(617) 542-5679
Gay and lesbian fiction and nonfiction.

Aunt Lute Books
(415) 826-1300
Lesbian fiction and nonfiction

Beacon Press
(617) 742-2110
Gay and lesbian nonfiction

Firebrand Books
(607) 272-0000
Lesbian and bisexual women's fiction, nonfiction, erotica, and poetry.

Haworth Press/Harrington Park Press
(607) 722-5857
Mainstream press with a gay and lesbian division

Naid Press
(904) 539-5965
Lesbian fiction, nonfiction, erotica, academic, and historical subjects.

SAGE Publications
(805) 499-0721
Gay and lesbian division-scholarly, health

Spinsters, Ink
(218)727-3222
Feminist fiction, nonfiction, political and contemporary issues and themes.

Bookstores

A Different Light—Order By Phone: (800) 343-4002

A Different Light—New York, NY: (212) 989-4850

A Different Light—San Francisco, CA: (415) 431-0891

A Different Light—West Hollywood, CA: (310) 854-6601

Lambda Rising—Order by Phone: (800) 621-6969

Lambda Rising—Washington DC: (202) 462-6969

✑ Appendix B
Organizations, Hotlines, and Resources

*T*he resources available for lesbians and bisexual women, their families, and their health professionals are overwhelming. Listed here are at least two resources in each category. If the resources chosen are not local, contacting national organizations or the resources from other parts of the country will be helpful in steering readers to local supports. Local gay and lesbian bookstores are also a good place to find resources (some are listed in Appendix A). Finally, the Internet has hundreds of resources for information or support. Listing "lesbian" or "bisexual" through any search engine will result in a vast number of resources.

National Organizations—General

Gay and Lesbian Medical Association (GLMA)—San Francisco, CA: (415) 255-4547

National Lesbian and Gay Health Association—Washington, DC: (202) 939-7880

The National Gay and Lesbian Task Force—Washington, DC: (202) 332-6483

Human Rights Campaign—Washington, DC: (202) 628-4160

Gay and Lesbian National Hotline: 888-843-4564 (888-THE-GLNH)

Parents and Friends of Lesbians and Gays (PFLAG)—Washington, DC (national office): (202) 638-4200

Legal Organizations

Lambda Legal Defense and Education Fund—New York, NY: (212) 995-8585

National Center for Lesbian Rights—San Francisco, CA: (415) 392-6257

Regional Organizations or Clinics

Howard Brown Health Center—Chicago, IL: (773) 388-1600

Community Health Project—New York, NY: (212) 675-3559

Lyon Martin Women's Health Clinic—San Francisco, CA: (415) 525-7312

Atlanta Gay and Lesbian Center—Atlanta, GA: (404) 876-5372 hotline: (404) 892-0661

New York City Lesbian and Gay Services Center—New York, NY: (212) 620-7310

Families and Couples

Alternative Family Project—San Francisco, CA: (415) 436-9000

Lesbian and Gay Parenting Project (c/o Lyon Martin Clinic)— San Francisco, CA: (415) 525-7312

Lavender Families Resource Network—Seattle, WA: (206) 325-2643

Center Kids—The Family Project—New York, NY: (212) 620-7310

Partners Task Force for Gay and Lesbian Couples—Seattle, WA: (206) 935-1206

Love Makes a Family—Portland, OR: (503) 228-3892

Cultural Groups and Support Groups

Elderly

Lesbian and Gay Aging Issue Network—San Francisco, CA:
(415) 974-9600

National Association for Gay and Lesbian Gerontology—San Francisco,
CA: 1290 Sutter Street, Suite 8, San Francisco, CA 94109

Senior Action in a Gay Environment (SAGE)—New York, NY:
(212) 741-2247

Youth

Lavender Youth Recreation and Information Center (LYRIC)—
San Francisco, CA: (415) 703-6150, 703-6161 or 1-800-246-pride youth
talk line

Richmond Organization for Sexual Minority Youth—Richmond, VA:
Youth Support (804) 353-2077, Office: (804) 353-1699

Hetrick-Martin Institute and the Harvey Milk School—New York, NY:
(212) 674-2600, TTY: (212) 633-8926

People With Disabilities

Communication Access Network (Deaf S/M)—San Francisco, CA:
(415) 431-5385 voice, TTY: (415) 431-5384

Deaf Gay and Lesbian Center—San Francisco, CA: TTY:
(415) 255-0700 TTY

Dykes with Disabilities (newsletter)—PO Box 1722, Madison, WI 53701-
1722

People of Color

Black Gay and Lesbian Leadership Forum—Los Angeles, CA:
(213) 964-7820

National Black Lesbian and Gay Leadership Forum—Washington, DC: (202) 483-6786

Asian Pacific Lesbian and Bisexual Women's Network (National): (510) 814-2422

Queer Asian Pacific Alliance—Boston, MA: (617) 499-9531

Asians & Friends—Dallas, TX: (214) 392-3339

Trikone: Gay & Lesbian South Asians—Los Angeles, CA: (213) 993-7626

Asociacion Gay/Lesbian Unida Impactando Latinos as A Superarse— San Francisco, CA: (415) 285-8405

S/M

Arizona Power Exchange: P O Box 67532, Phoenix, AZ 85082-7532

National Leather Association (NLA): PO Box 2844, Southfield, MI 48037-2844

NLA Florida: PO Box 4911, Ft. Lauderdale, FL 33338-4911

Woman Link: 2124 Kittredge, #257, Berkeley, CA 94704

The Exiles—San Francisco, CA: (415) 487-5170

Bisexual

BiNet USA: P.O. Box 7327 Langley Park, MD 20787

Bisexual Resources Center—Cambridge, MA: (617) 424-9595

Health Specific

Cancer

National Coalition of Feminist and Lesbian Cancer Project and the Mary-Helen Mautner Project for Lesbians with Cancer—Washington, DC: (202) 332-5536

Lesbian Community Cancer Project—Chicago, IL: (312) 561-4662

Domestic Violence and Hate Violence

Lesbian Services Program of Woman, Inc.—San Francisco, CA: (415) 864-4722 (domestic violence)

Community United Against Violence (CUAV)—San Francisco, CA: (415) 777-5500 (domestic and hate violence)

New York City Gay and Lesbian Anti-Violence Project—New York, NY: Hotline (212) 807-0197 (domestic and hate violence)

Advocates for Abused and Battered Lesbians: (206) 547-8191 (domestic violence)

HIV/AIDS

Lesbian AIDS Project (LAP) c/o Gay Men's Health Crisis—New York, NY: (212) 367-1000

Mental Health and Substance Use

New Leaf—San Francisco, CA: (415) 626-7000

Out and Free (Quit Tobacco Program): 1-888-820-1821

The Alliance of Psychological Health Care Professionals—San Diego, CA: (619) 683-8000

Lifecourse Counseling Center: (413) 253-2822

Appendix C
Methodological Considerations

$\mathcal{I}$t is critical to realize the methodological considerations of lesbian and bisexual health research prior to understanding the implications of the results. These considerations include a constantly changing community and the inability to obtain a probability sample. In addition, universal definitions and categories have not yet been established in this emerging field. Finally, the descriptive univariate and bivariate statistics generally presented in this research are highly sensitive to sampling bias.

A CHANGING POPULATION

Lesbians and bisexual women are finally becoming visible in the fight for human rights. As this struggle becomes more intense and public, the treatment of lesbians and bisexual women by the mainstream, as well as the treatment of diversity within the lesbian and bisexual community is in constant flux. It is likely that these changes are reflected in health-related behaviors and the health care treatment of these women. Therefore, research conducted in the past may not accurately reflect current concerns. It is important for lesbian and bisexual women's health researchers and their audiences to question and address assumptions based on past research.

✂ SAMPLING METHODOLOGY

One of the biggest obstacles in community-based research is obtaining a representative sample. In order to obtain a representative sample of a population, the parameters of this population must be known. Whenever a lesbian or bisexual woman discloses her sexual orientation, there is risk of discrimination. Therefore, many women who self-identify as lesbian or bisexual are unwilling to disclose their identity and/or their sexual behavior. This, in conjunction with the fact that they are not definitely recognizable by their appearance or through medical tests, and the fact that they are represented in every geographic area, ethnicity, socioeconomic status, and generation, makes representative sampling impossible. Therefore, researchers are forced to rely on samples based on the self-disclosure of the participants.

Most lesbians and bisexual health researchers recruit subjects through networks available in the lesbian and bisexual women's community, such as at lesbian, gay, and bisexual organizations, mailing lists, events, bars, and businesses frequented by members of this community. Some researchers choose to recruit through several different organizations, while others recruit at one event. Researchers may target only lesbian or bisexual populations or attempt to recruit heterosexual controls. Regardless of the recruitment methodology, until lesbians and bisexual women feel free to disclose their sexual orientation, probability sampling will remain impossible.

This bias does not invalidate the results, rather it confines the results to a specific population. For example, if subjects are drawn from a sample of lesbians and bisexual women frequenting a gay and lesbian event in San Francisco, then we can assume the results are true for at least this population and hypothesize, with additional information from other studies, whether the results generalize to other subgroups of lesbians and bisexual women. It is critical when examining research to pay close attention to the sampling methodology of each study and look for patterns in results. If patterns emerge in results of multiple studies with different recruitment strategies, the population for whom the results are valid expand. However, research will always be missing the women who are not willing to disclose their sexual orientation or same-sex sexual behavior, therefore, the results will not be generalizable to the entire population of lesbians and bisexual women until lesbians and bisexual women no longer fear discrimination.

Another significant problem in the samples used in lesbian and bisexual women's health research is the underrepresentation of women of color, poor women, women living in rural areas, women over 60, and transgendered women. Although race, ethnicity, education level, socioeconomic status, geographic area, and age are important factors in health and health care, little research has examined the effects of demographic differences on the health and health care of lesbians and bisexual women.

Future health research specifically targeting or oversampling elderly lesbians and bisexual women, lesbians and bisexual women with disabilities, lesbians and bisexual women of color, lesbians and bisexual women living in poverty, and transgendered women are clearly needed.

✑ LACK OF UNIVERSAL DEFINITIONS AND CATEGORIES

The lack of universal terms and definitions in lesbian and bisexual women's health research makes it difficult to compare studies and to detect overall patterns. One of the most complex definitions is that of the lesbian or bisexual woman. As discussed throughout the book, behaviors do not necessarily correspond to common definitions of identity and vice versa (i.e., a woman identifying as a lesbian may have sexual relationships with a man). Furthermore, individual identity is fluid and dynamic, rather than fixed. Some researchers, particularly those interested in sexual behavior, define lesbians as women who have sexual relationships with women, and bisexuals as women who have sexual relationships with both men and women. Others choose to focus on the woman's self-identity. Therefore, the results being compared are for, in all practicalities, two separate samples.

These methodological considerations do not invalidate the results of lesbian and bisexual women's health. It is important to focus on patterns, using the results of individual studies as typical examples. The review of the research presented in Chapter 1 shows some of the patterns of the health problems and health concerns of lesbians and bisexual women.

❧ Appendix D
Forms and Interviewing

❧ FORMS

Forms are one of the first things patients see when they visit a new health care professional. Often, lesbians, bisexual, and transsexual women do not fit neatly within the categories offered on the forms, putting them in the position of either creating new categories, leaving answers blank (and perhaps having to explain why), or lying about themselves and their partners. This can leave them feeling angry, confused, and uncomfortable prior to ever seeing the provider. By contrast, well thought out forms can create positive feelings where the lesbian, bisexual, or transsexual woman feels accepted and respected.

Reading the descriptions of the women below and filling out the questions from her perspective may help you understand the importance of appropriate questions on forms. Think about how it might make her feel as she fills them out, what it might do to her relationship with the provider who will be seeing her, and what information this provider will miss from the way in which the question is worded.

Lee

Lee, a self-identified lesbian, is in a long-term, monogamous relationship with a female partner. She goes for a gynecological exam for the first time in 15 years at her HMO. She is not interested in getting pregnant.

1. **Sex**   male   female

2. **Marital status**   single   married   divorced   widowed

3. **Are you sexually active?**   yes   no

4. **If yes, what birth control do you use?** _____

Lee gets stuck when she tries to answer her marital status. She is in a long-term, marriage-like relationship, but she does not have the legal benefits of marriage, including being covered on her partner's health insurance plan. If she circles "married" the provider will probably assume that she has a husband with all the privileges that encompasses. On the other hand, if she circles "single," she is not acknowledging her long-term partner and may have a difficult time incorporating this woman in her care. Besides, her lifestyle is more like that of a heterosexual married woman than that of a single woman. She also gets stuck on the next two questions. She is sexually active, but birth control is unnecessary because she is active with women. Question 4 assumes that women who are sexually active should use birth control. Providers often encourage women (sometimes insistently) who are sexually active to agree to some type of birth control. Lee probably knows that this is a potential confrontation. She may choose to come out to her provider by filling in information about the sex of her partner; however, because the forms are so obviously designed for the heterosexual, she is likely to feel uncomfortable doing this.

Amy

Amy, a 25-year-old transsexual, was born with male anatomy but realized at the age of 17 that she could not live her life as a man. She began taking hormones at the age of 22, had breast implants at the age of 23, and was currently saving money for vaginal construction. She fills out an intake form prior to visiting a physician at a women's health clinic. She is in a relationship with a woman and considers herself to be a lesbian.

1. **Sex**   male   female

2. **Marital status**   single   married   divorced   widowed

3. **Are you sexually active?**   yes   no

4. **If yes, what birth control do you use?** _____

5. **Sexual orientation**   lesbian   bisexual   heterosexual

Amy gets stuck on the first question. She identifies as a woman, but she knows that her health provider would then assume that she has a vagina with all the health concerns of a biologically born woman. More accurately, she is a male to female transsexual. This question assumes that everyone fits the dichotomy of male and female. Like Lee she can not accurately fill out her marital status either. The next two questions on birth control will only confuse the people reading the forms, because although she still has a penis, she chooses not to engage in vaginal-penile intercourse. Finally, she identifies herself as a lesbian in the last question, although she is sure that that will raise questions when they find out about her transsexualism.

Cassandra

Cassandra is in a relationship with a female to male transsexual who was in the process of transitioning. They started the relationship before her partner even thought about becoming a man. For the first five years of her relationship, she identified herself as a lesbian, actively participating in the lesbian community. She fills out this intake form prior to a gynecological visit.

1. **Sex**   male   female

2. **Marital status**   single   married   divorced   widowed

3. **Sexual orientation**   lesbian   bisexual   heterosexual

4. **Do you have sex with**   men   women   both   neither

Cassandra gets stuck on the sexual orientation question and on the question about the sex of her partner. She needs blank spaces where she can specify the complexity of her situation. She leaves both questions blank.

Suggestions

1. Look through the form and make sure that there are no assumptions about gender (e.g., husband/wife, mother/father, pronouns— what is *his* occupation).

2. Whenever you have sex or gender in a question, add a third category for transgender with a blank after it so that the individual can specify their particular circumstance.

3. For questions on marital status or relationship status include either living in a marriage type relationship or domestic partner. You may want to ask the sex of the partner.

4. Questions about families should allow for alternative families, including two parents of the same sex and more than two parents.

5. Include as many categories as space permits, this way as many people as possible will feel represented.

6. For any question where there are possible other answers, leave an "other" category with space for them to specify.

7. Make it clear on the form how confidentiality will be protected and who has access to the information. Always offer the patient the right to refuse to answer a question.

✂ INTERVIEWING

Similarly, in interviews and history taking, standard questions are often inappropriate for the lesbian, bisexual, or transsexual woman. Here the health professional has control over what questions to ask and what not to ask, the terminology to use (including but not limited to pronouns), and how to diffuse the situation if the patient becomes uncomfortable. The health care provider should think carefully about what information is relevant and make sure that the initial questions are open-ended enough for the patient to answer truthfully without having to correct the provider. Remember, with the power dynamics of the provider-patient relationship, it is often difficult for the patient to correct a false assumption by her doctor.

Suggestions

1. Make no assumptions. Every woman who walks into a provider's office can self-identify as a lesbian and/or have had relationships with women. Similarly she may have been born a man. And this can change over time. Make sure that you ask these questions of everyone for the past and present and ask them again over time.

2. Spend time thinking about the questions that are important and why. Think about what you will ask after particular responses. Be as specific as necessary.

3. Apologize if she seems offended. Explain (briefly) that you need the information to provide her with the best possible care. Ask what terminology she may prefer (i.e., if you call her partner a lover and she seems offended ask what she usually calls her).

4. You must be completely comfortable talking about sex (slang and technical). Practice with friends. Read books on the topics that make you the most uncomfortable (i.e., same-sex sexuality, s/m). Look at pictures, watch movies. The more comfortable you are the more comfortable your patients will be. Humor (in good taste) is often a helpful relief.

5. Condemning is not helpful. You have a right to your own morals and beliefs in your personal life, but not in your professional life. If you are not comfortable with particular behaviors, lifestyles, or orientations, admit it to yourself and try to refer your patient to someone who can serve them better. Patients will most likely pick up, in the interview, negative attitudes.

6. Once again, make clear how her confidentiality will be protected, who will have access to the information, etc. Give her the option of refusing to answer a question (if her confidentiality cannot be protected, it may be to her disadvantage to provide specific information about her sexuality).

7. When questioning a person who has been hurt during sexual play, be particularly sensitive.

8. Learn as much about as many different cultures as possible, and their ways of understanding and thinking about sexuality.

Suggested Questions
(Forms and/or Interviews)

1. **Sex**   male   female   trangender (please specify _____)

2. **Relationship status**   legally married   marriage-type relationship
   divorced   separated   widowed   single
   other (please specify _____)

3. **Sex of partner**   male   female   transgender
   (please specify _____)

4. **Are you sexually active?**   yes   no

5. **Is birth control necessary?**   yes   no, why not? _____

   _____

6. **Do you use birth control?**   no   yes, what type?

   _____

7. **Sexual orientation**   lesbian/gay   bisexual   heterosexual
   other (please specify _____)

8. **Sex of partner(s)?**   men   women   both   neither
   transgender (please specify _____)

References

Aarons, L. (1995). *Prayers for Bobby*. San Francisco: Harper San Francisco.

Anderson, C. W., & Smith, H. (1993). Stigma and honor: Gay, lesbian, and bisexual people in the U.S. military. In L. Diamant (Ed.), *Homosexual issues in the workplace. Series in clinical and community psychology* (pp. 65-89). Washington, DC: Taylor & Francis.

Banks, A., & Gartrell, N. K. (1996). Lesbians in the medical setting. In R. P. Cajab & T. S. Stein (Eds.), *Textbook of homosexuality and mental health* (pp. 659-671). Washington, DC: American Psychiatric Press.

Blumenfeld, W. (1988). *Looking at gay and lesbian life*. Boston: Beacon Press.

Booth, L. (1995). Spirituality and the gay community. *Journal of Gay and Lesbian Social Services, 2*(1), 57-65.

Bradford, J., & Ryan, C. (1988). *The national lesbian health care survey*. Washington, DC: National Gay and Lesbian Health Foundation.

Bradford, J., Ryan, C., & Rothblum, E. D. (1994). National lesbian health care survey: Implications for mental health care. *Journal of Consulting and Clinical Psychology, 62*(2), 228-242.

Buenting, J. A. (1992). Health life-styles of lesbian and heterosexual women. *Health Care for Women International, 13*(2), 165-171.

Bybee, D. (1991). *The Michigan lesbian health report*. Michigan: Michigan Organization for Human Rights.

Califia, P., & Sweeney, R. (1996). Safer sex guidelines for leather dykes. In P. Califia & R. Sweeney (Eds.), *The second coming: A leatherdyke reader* (pp. 351-354). Los Angeles: Alyson Publications.

Cass, V. (1984). Homosexual identity formation: Testing a theoretical model. *Journal of Sex Research, 20*, 143-167.

Cass, V. (1996). Sexual orientation identity formation: A western phenomenon. In R. P. Cabaj & T. S. Stein (Eds.), *Textbook of homosexuality and mental health* (pp. 227-252). Washington, DC: American Psychiatric Press.

Cass, V. C. (1979). Homosexual identity formation: A theoretical model. *Journal of Homosexuality, 5*(3), 219-235.

Chan, C. S. (1993). Issues of identity development among Asian-American lesbians and gay men. In L. D. Garnets & D. C. Kimmel (Eds.), *Psychological perspectives on lesbian and gay male experiences* (pp. 376-387). New York: Columbia University Press.

173

Chng, C., Havens, J., & Fasick, J. (1990). *Lesbians and HIV infection: A community based study.* Dallas, TX: Nelson-Tebedo Community Clinic for AIDS Research.

Chu, S., Hammett, T., & Beuhler, J. (1992). Update: Epidemiology of reported cases of AIDS in women who report sex only with women. United States, 1980-1991 (letter). *Aids, 6,* 518-519.

Cochran, S. D., & Mays, V. M. (1988). Disclosure of sexual preference to physicians by black lesbians and bisexual women. *Western Journal of Medicine, 149,* 616-619.

Coleman, E. (1981). Developmental stages of the coming out process. *Journal of Homosexuality, 7,* 31-43.

Coleman, V. E. (1991). Violence between lesbian couples: A between groups comparison. *Dissertation Abstracts International, 51,* (n11-B):5634-5635.

Cox, S., & Gallois, C. (1996). Gay and lesbian identity development: A social identity perspective. *Journal of Homosexuality, 30*(4), 1-30.

Curry, H., Clifford, D., & Leonard, R. (1994). *A legal guide for lesbian and gay couples.* (8th ed.). Berkeley, CA: Nolo Press.

Dardick, L., & Grady, K. (1980). Openness between gay persons and health professionals. *Annals of Internal Medicine, 93,* 115-119.

D'Augelli, A., & Hershberger, S. (1993). Lesbian, gay and bisexual youth in community settings: Personal challenges and mental health problems. *American Journal of Community Psychology, 21,* 421-448.

Deevey, S. (1990). Older lesbian women: An invisible minority. *Journal of Gerontological Nursing, 16*(5), 35-39.

Deevey, S. (1993). Lesbian self-disclosure. Strategies for success [see comments]. *Journal of Psychosocial Nursing and Mental Health Services, 31*(4), 21-26.

Denenberg, R. (1994). *Report on lesbian health.* Washington, D.C.: National Gay and Lesbian Task Force Policy Institute.

Einhorn, L., & Polgar, M. (1994). HIV-risk behavior among lesbians and bisexual women. *AIDS Education and Prevention, 6* (514-523).

Elliot, P. (1996). Shattering illusions: Same-sex domestic violence. In C. M. Renzetti & C. H. Miley (Eds.), *Violence in gay and lesbian domestic partnerships* (pp. 1-8). Binghamton, NY: Harrington Park Press.

EMT Associates. (1991). *Gay men, lesbians and their alcohol and other drug use: San Francisco.* San Francisco: Lesbian And Gay Substance Planning Group.

Espin, O. M. (1993). Issues of identity in the psychology of Latin lesbians. In L. D. Garnets & D. C. Kimmel (Eds.), *Psychological perspectives on lesbian and gay male experiences* (pp. 348-363). New York: Columbia University Press.

Ettelbrick, P. L. (1996). Legal issues in health care for lesbians and gay men. In K. J. Peterson (Ed.), *Health care for lesbians and gay men: Confronting homophobia and heterosexism* (pp. 93-109). New York: Harrington Park Press.

Falco, K. L. (1996). Psychotherapy with women who love women. In R. P. Cabaj & T. S. Stein (Eds.), *Textbook of homosexuality and mental health* (pp. 397-412). Washington, DC: American Psychiatric Press.

Flaks, D. K., Ficher, I., Masterpasqua, F., & Joseph, G. (1995). Lesbians choosing motherhood: A comparative study of lesbian and heterosexual parents and their children. *Developmental Psychology, 31*(1), 105-114.

Garnets, L., Hancock, K. A., Cochran, S. D., Goodchilds, J. et al. (1991). Issues in psychotherapy with lesbians and gay men: A survey of psychologists. *American Psychologist, 46*(9), 964-972.

Garnets, L. D., & Kimmel, D. C. (Eds.). (1993). *Psychological perspectives on lesbian and gay male experiences.* New York: Columbia University Press.

Gibson, P. (1989). Gay male and lesbian youth suicide. Report of secretary's task force on youth suicide (Publication No. ADM-89-1623, Vol. 3). Washington, DC: ADAMHA CDHHS.

Golombok, S., Spencer, A., & Rotter, M. (1983). Children in lesbian and single-parent households: Psychosexual and psychiatric appraisal. *Journal of Child Psychology and Psychiatry, 24,* 551-572.

Golombok, S., & Tasker, F. (1996). Do parents influence the sexual orientation of their children? Findings from a longitudinal study of lesbian families. *Developmental Psychology, 32*(1), 3-11.

Gonsiorek, J. C. (1993). Mental health issues of gay and lesbian adolescents. In L. D. Garnets & D. C. Kimmel (Eds.), *Psychological perspectives on lesbian and gay male experiences* (pp. 348-363). New York: Columbia University Press.

Gonzalez, F. J., & Espin, O. M. (Eds.). (1996). *Latino man, Latina women, and homosexuality.* Washington, DC: American Psychiatric Press.

Gottman, J. S. (1990). Children of gay and lesbian parents. In F. W. Bozett & M. B. Sussman (Eds.), *Homosexuality and family relations* (pp. 177-196). New York: Harrington Park Press.

Green, R., Mandel, J., Hotvedt, M., Gray, & Smith, L. (1986). Lesbian mothers and their children: A comparison with solo parents, heterosexual mothers, and their children. *Archives of Sexual Behavior, 15,* 167-184.

Greene, B. (1994). Ethnic-minority lesbians and gay men: Mental health and treatment issues. *Journal of Consulting and Clinical Psychology, 62*(2), 243-251.

Gruskin, E. P. (1995). *The contra costa lesbian/bisexual women's health study.* Unpublished master's thesis, University of California, Berkeley.

Harrison, A. E. (1996). Comprehensive care of lesbian and gay families. *Primary Care, 23*(1), 31-55.

Herdt, G., & Boxer, A. (1993). *Children of the horizons: How gay and lesbian teens are leading a new way out of the closet.* Boston: Beacon Press.

Herek, G. (1992). Psychological heterosexism and anti-gay violence: The social psychology of bigotry and bashing. In G. Herek & K. Berrill (Eds.), *Hate crimes: Confronting violence against lesbians and gay men* (pp. 149-169). Newbury Park, CA: Sage Publications.

Herek, G., & Berrill, K. (Eds.). (1992). *Hate crimes: Confronting violence against lesbians and gay men.* Newbury Park, CA: Sage Publications.

Herek, G. M. (1997). The HIV epidemic and public attitudes toward lesbians and gay men. In M. P. Levine, P. M. Nardi, & J. H. Gagnon (Eds.), *In changing times: Gay men and lesbians encounter HIV/AIDS* (pp. 191-218). Chicago: University of Chicago Press.

Herman, E. (1995). *Psychiatry, psychology, and homosexuality.* New York: Chelsea House Publishers.

Hitchcock, J. M., & Wilson, H. S. (1992). Personal risking: Lesbian self-disclosure of sexual orientation to professional health care providers. *Nursing Research, 41*(3), 178-183.

Huggins, S. (1989). A comparative study of self-esteem of adolescent children of divorced lesbian mothers and divorced heterosexual mothers. In F. Bozett (Ed.), *Homosexuality and the family* (pp. 123-135). New York: Harrington Park Press.

Hunter, J. (1992). Violence against lesbians and gay male youths.In G. Herek & K. Berrill (Eds.), *Hate crimes: Confronting violence against lesbians and gay men* (pp. 76-82). Newbury Park, CA: Sage Publications.

Hutchins, L., & Ka'ahumanu, L. (Eds.). (1991). *Bi Any Other Name: Bisexual People Speak Out.* Boston: Alyson.

Jack, D. C. (1991). *Silencing the self: Women and depression.* Cambridge, MA: Harvard University Press.

Jones, B. E., & Hill, M. J. (1996). African American lesbians, gay men, and bisexuals. In R. P. Cabaj & T. S. Stein (Eds.), *Textbook of homosexuality and mental health* (pp. 549-561). Washington, D.C.: American Psychiatric Press.

Jones, F. D., & Koshes, R. J. (1995). Homosexuality and the military. *American Journal of Psychiatry, 152*(1), 16-21.

Kendall, K. (1995). *Legal issues pertinent to gays and lesbians* [Lecture]. Presented to lesbian, gay, bisexual, and transgender health and culture course, School of Public Health, University of California, Berkeley.

Kinsey, A., Pomeroy, W., & Martin, C. (1948). *Sexual behavior in the human male.* Philadelphia: WB Saunders.

Kinsey, A., Pomeroy, W., & Martin, C. (1953). *Sexual behavior in the human female.* Philadelphia: WB Saunders.

Kirkpartrick, M., Smith, C., & Roy, R. (1981). Lesbian mothers and their children: A comparative survey. *American Journal of Orthopsychiatry, 51,* 545-551.

Kleinberg, L. H. (1986). Psychological experiences associated with lesbian identity disclosure to parents: An exploratory study. *Dissertation Abstracts International, 47,* (n3-B):1329.

Krajeski, J. (1996). Homosexuality and the mental health professions: A contemporary history. In R. P. Cabaj & T. S. Stein (Eds.), *A textbook of homosexuality and mental health.* Washington, D.C.: American Psychiatric Press.

Meyer, C. L. (1992). Legal, psychological, and medical considerations in lesbian parenting. *Law and Sexuality, 2,* 237-264.

Monzon, O., & Capellan, J. (1987). Female-to-female transmission of HIV (letter). *Lancet, 2,* 40-41.

Murphy, B. C. (1989). Lesbian couples and their parents: The effects of perceived parental attitudes on the couples [Special Issue]. *Journal of Counseling & Development, 68*(1), 46-51.

Nakajima, Q. A., Chan, Y. H., & Lee, K. (1996). Mental health issues for gay and lesbian Asian Americans. In R. P. Cabaj & T. S. Stein (Eds.), *Textbook of homosexuality and mental health* (pp. 563-581). Washington, DC: American Psychiatric Press.

National Coalition of Anti-Violence Programs and Community United Against Violence. (1996). *Anti-lesbian/gay violence in 1995.* San Francisco: Author.

O'Hanlan, K. (1995, July/August). Lesbian health and homophobia: Perspectives for the treating obstetrician/gynecologist. *Current Problems in Obstetrics, Gynecology, and Fertility,* 97-133.

O'Hanlan, K. A. (1996). *Gay and lesbian health issues: An academic review of survey demography, apparent risks for cancers and heart disease, effects of societal, medical and governmental bias, and a call for higher standard of medical fairness.* Paper presented at the International Society for Medical Ethics, San Francisco.

Patterson, C. J. (1992). Children of lesbian and gay parents. *Child Development, 63*(5), 1025-1042.

Paul, J. (1986). *Growing up with a gay, lesbian, or bisexual parent: An exploratory study of experiences and perceptions.* Unpublished doctoral dissertation, University of California, Berkeley.

Perrin, E. C., & Kulkin, H. (1996). Pediatric care for children whose parents are gay or lesbian. *Pediatrics, 97*(5), 629-635.

Peterson, K. J. (Ed.). (1996). *Health care for lesbians and gay men: Confronting homophobia and heterosexism.* New York: Harrington Park Press.

Pies, C. (1985). *Considering parenthood.* San Francisco: Spinsters/Aunt Lute.

Ponse, B. R. (1977). Identities in the lesbian world. *Dissertation Abstracts International, 38,* (n1-A):504.

Purcell, D. W., & Hicks, D. W. (1996). Institutional discrimination against lesbians, gay men, and bisexuals. In R. Cabaj & T. Stein (Eds.), *A textbook on homosexuality and mental health* (pp. 763-782). Washington, DC: American Psychiatric Press.

Puryear, D. (1983). *A comparison between the children of lesbian mothers and the children of heterosexual mothers.* Unpublished doctoral dissertation, University of California, Berkeley.

Randall, C. (1989). Lesbian phobia among BSN educators: A survey. *Journal of Nursing Education, 28,* 302-306.

Robertson, M. M. (1992). Lesbians as an invisible minority in the health services arena. *Health Care for Women International, 13*(2), 155-163.

Ross, M., Paulsen, J., & Stalstrom, O. (1988). Homosexuality and mental health: A cross cultural review. *Journal of Homosexuality, 15,* 131-152.

Roter, D. L., & Hall, J. A. (1992). *Doctors talking with patients: Patients talking with doctors.* Westport, CT: Auburn House.

Schatz, B., & O'Hanlan, K. (1994). *Anti-gay discrimination in medicine: Results of a national survey of Lesbian, Gay and Bisexual Physicians.* San Francisco: American Association of Lesbian and Gay Physicians.

Schneider, M. (1989). Sappho was a right-on adolescent: Growing up lesbian [Special Issue]. *Journal of Homosexuality, 17*(1-2), 111-130.

Silverstein, C. (1996). History of treatment. In R. P. Cabaj & T. S. Stein (Eds.), *A textbook of homosexuality and mental health*. Washington, D.C.: American Psychiatric Press.

Stevens, P. A., & Hall, J. M. (1993). Stigma, health beliefs, and experiences with health care in lesbian women. *Image: Journal of Nursing Scholarship, 20*(2), 69-73.

Stevens, P. E. (1992). Lesbian health care research: a review of the literature from 1970 to 1990. *Health Care for Women International, 13*(2), 91-120.

Stevens, P. E. (1993). Lesbians and HIV: Clinical research and policy issues. *American Journal of Orthopsychiatry, 63*(2), 289-94.

Stevens, P. E., & Hall, J. M. (1990). Abusive health care interactions experienced by lesbians: A case of institutional violence in the treatment of women. *Response to the Victimization of Women and Children, 13*(3), 23-27.

Strommen, E. F. (1989). "You're a what?": Family member reactions to the disclosure of homosexuality. In L. D. Garnets & D. C. Kimmel (Eds.), *Psychological perspectives on lesbian and gay male experiences* (pp. 248-266). New York: Columbia University Press.

Stryker, S. (1994). *Transgender health* [Lecture]. Presented to lesbian, gay, bisexual, and transgender health and culture course. School of Public Health, University of California, Berkeley.

Tafoya, T. N. (1996). Native two-spirited people. In R. P. Cabaj & T. S. Stein (Eds.), *A textbook of homosexuality and mental health* (pp. 603-617). Washington, D.C.: American Psychiatric Press, Inc.

Troiden, R. (1989). The formation of homosexual identities. *Journal of Homosexuality, 14*, 43-73.

Troiden, R. R. (1993). The formation of homosexual identities. In L. D. Garnets & D. C. Kimmel (Eds.), *Psychological perspectives on lesbian and gay male experiences* (pp. 191-217). New York: Columbia University Press.

Von Schulthess, B. (1992). Violence in the streets: Anti-lesbian assault and harassment in San Francisco. In G. Herek & K. Berrill (Eds.), *Hate crimes: Confronting violence against lesbians and gay men* (pp. 65-73). Newbury Park, CA: Sage Publications.

Waitzkin, H. (1991). *The Politics of the Medical Encounter*. New Haven, NJ: Yale University Press.

Wallick, M. M., Cambre, K. M., & Townsend, M. H. (1992). How the topic of homosexuality is taught at U.S. medical schools. *Academic Medicine, 67*(9), 601-603.

Weinberg, M. S., Williams, C. J., & Pryor, D. W. (1994). *Dual attraction: Understanding bisexuality*. New York: Oxford University Press.

White, J., & Levinson, W. (1993). Primary care of lesbian patients. *Journal of General Internal Medicine, 8*(1), 41-47.

Zeidenstein, L. (1990). Gynecological and childbearing needs of lesbians. *Journal of Nurse-Midwifery, 35*(1), 10-18.

✎ Author Index

⤜ Subject Index

✺ About the Author

Elisabeth Paige Gruskin has been helping sensitize people toward the needs of the lesbian and bisexual community for the past five years. She has a doctoral degree from the University of California at Berkeley, where she developed and taught six semesters of a graduate class entitled "Lesbian, Gay, Bisexual, and Transgender Health and Culture." She has spoken at more than a dozen national conferences and has lectured all over Northern California on lesbian and gay health issues. She is currently a research associate at the Division of Research at Kaiser Permanente Medical Care, one of the nation's largest health maintenance organizations. She is working on a project concerning the health effects of sexual orientation on female members of a large HMO, funded in part by the Lesbian Health Fund from the National Gay and Lesbian Medical Association. She is also a fellow at the Health Policy Institute at the University of California, San Francisco.